J. B. Parsons

Patriotic Roster of LaSalle County, Illinois

J. B. Parsons

Patriotic Roster of LaSalle County, Illinois

ISBN/EAN: 9783337306564

Printed in Europe, USA, Canada, Australia, Japan

Cover: Foto ©ninafisch / pixelio.de

More available books at **www.hansebooks.com**

Patriotic Roster

-OF-

La Salle County,

Illinois.

Compiled and Published by

J. B. PARSONS,

Pontiac, Ill.

Late Sergt. Co. A. 1st Maine H. A.
Late Col. 10th Inf. I. N. G.
Late Aide-de-camp to Nat'l Com. G. A. R.

1899.
Price 25 Cents.

1912818

OTTAWA.

Seth C. Earl Post 156, G. A. R.

OTTAWA, ILL.

Organized Sept. 25th, 1882.

OFFICERS.

R. C. JORDAN..........................Commander
R. D. McDONALD...........Senior Vice-Commander
WILLIAM JENCKS..........Junior Vice-Commander
J. C. PETTIT.................................Surgeon
WILLIAM BURGESS.......................Chaplain
F. M. SAPP...............................Adjutant
DAVID KROUSE.....................Quartermaster
J. W. HARNER...................Officer of the Day
S. B. BATHURST................Officer of the Guard
JACOB CHRISTMANN.................Sergeant Major
J. H. WATSON........................Q. M. Sergeant
D. B. SNOW........................Judge Advocate

PAST POST COMMANDERS.

E. A. SMITH
T. C. GIBSON
E. A. NATTINGER
D. A. COOK
M. HANIFEN
DAVID KROUSE
WILLIAM BURGESS
JACOB BANE

S. B. BATHURST
JOSEPH ENGOMAR
G. H. ROBERTS
F. M. SAPP
D. B. SNOW
D. HAPEMAN
W. K. STEWART
L. W. BREWER

MEMBERS.

Acton, G. C., Bugler Co. D, 2d Neb. Cav.
Anderson, James, Private Co. H, 11th Ill. Inf.
Armstrong, W. S., Color Sergeant Co. H, 11th Ill. Inf.
Ayers, Oscar, Private, Henshaw's Battery.

(Seth C. Earl Post, Ottawa, Illinois, Continued.)

Baldwin, M. W., Leader of Band, 11th Ill. Inf.
Bane, Jacob, Private Co. I, 104th Ill. Inf.
Barrett, B. G., Co. K, 75th Ill. Inf.
Bartlett, Thomas, Private Co. G, 139th Ill. Inf.
Bathurst, S. B., Private Co. I, 54th Penn. Inf.
Beckwith, Daniel, Private Co. B, 53d Ill. Inf.
Baird, William, Private Co. A, 1st New Jersey Lt. Art.
Belknap, Augustus, Private Co. A, 64th Ill. Inf.
Bibbins, Joseph, Private Co. K, 5th N. Y. Heavy Art.
Bowermaster, G. W., Private Co. I, 31st Ohio Inf.
Boyd, John N., Corp. Co. K, 7th Penn. Cav.
Bradish, A. B, Capt. Co. I, 21st Wis. Inf.
Breese, J. H., Private Co. G, 1st Ill. Art.
Brewer, L. W., Corp. Co. I, 4th Ill. Cav.
Brush, C. H., Lt. Col. 53d Ill. Cav.
Burgess, William, Lieut. Cogswell's Battery.
Cain Thomas, Private Co. I, 1st Vet. N. Y. Cav.
Carpenter, P., Private Co. I, 1st Ill. Light Art.
Channel, John, Private Co. E, 5th Ill. Cav.
Carter, Justus, Private Co. D, 23d Ill. Inf.
Christmann, Jacob, Private Co. C, 4th Mo. Inf.
Clark, Josiah J., Private Co. E, 8th Conn Cav.
Condiff, J. B., Private Co. G, 41st Ill. Inf.
Condon, F. D., Private Co. C, 85th Penn. Inf.
Conant, H. O., Private Co. D, 1st Ohio Inf.
Cook, David A., Lieut. Co. B, 12th Ill. Inf.
Combs, J. R., Private Co. D, 127th Ill. Inf.
Costello, John, Private Co. C, 13th Mass. Inf.
Dreifuss, Max, Private Co. B, 8th Wis. Inf.
Duffy, C. C., Corp. Co. K, 105th Ill. Inf.
Ebersol, J. E. C., Corp. Co. I, 138th Ill. Inf.
Ehly, Adam, Private Co. C, 1st Ill. Light Art.
Engomar, Joseph, Sergt. Co. F, 46th Penn. Inf.
Eustis, John H., Private Co. A, 64th Ill. Inf.
Fuehe, G. W., Capt. Co. I, 24th Ill. Inf.
Ford, E. G., Private Co. B, 16th Maine Inf.
Foster, Charles, Private Co. D, 64th Ill. Inf.

(Seth C. Earl Post Ottawa, Illinois, Continued.)

Foster, E., Blacksmith Co. H, 1st Mich. Cav.
Frost, Frank, Co. A, 3d Ill. Cav.
Gibson, T. C., Major, 53d Ill. Inf.
Hapeman, Douglas, Lt. Col. 104th Ill. Inf.
Hanifen M., Private Co. B, 1st New Jersey Lt. Art.
Hanly, Patrick, Private Co. C, 59th Ill. Inf.
Hathaway, Stephen, Sergt. Co. A, 3d Mass. Inf.
Hazel, J. P., Corp. Co. C, 41st Ill. Inf.
Hill, John F., Private Co. C, 7th Ill. Cav.
Hillard, John, Private Co. C, 16th N Y. Inf.
Hoag, Charles, Private Co. A, 8th Ill Cav.
Horner, J. W., Private Co. C, 53d Ill. Inf.
Hossack, H. L., Capt. Co. I, 138th Ill. Inf.
Howard, T. J., Private Co. G, 8th Ill. Inf.
Holmes, Henry, Corp. Co. A, 53d Ill. Inf.
Harris, J. O., Sergeant, 53d Ill. Inf.
Jaka, John, Private Co. I, 9th Ill. Inf.
Jencks, William, Private Co. K, 129th Ill. Inf.
Johnston, Augustus, Private Co. I, 8th Ill. Cav.
Johnston, Peter, Private Co. H, 112th Ill. Inf.
Jones, Richard, Private Co. B, 62d Penn. Inf.
Jordan, R. C., Sergt. Co. K, 138th Ill. Inf.
Keim, Martin, Color Sergeant Co. I. 24th Ill. Inf.
King, Frank G, Capt. Co. C, 53d Ill. Inf.
Knapp, W. H., Private Co. A, 104th Ill. Inf.
Krouse, David, Corp. Co. G, 177th Penn. Inf.
Lawler, Patrick, Private, Henshaw's Battery.
Leland, Sherman, Sergt. Co. D, 104th Ill. Inf.
Lewis, George, Drummer Co. I, 104th Ill. Inf.
Locke, William, Sergt. Co. K, 13th Ind. Inf.
Lockwood, H. L., Private Co. I, 14th Ill. Cav.
Lyle, James, Private Co. E, 104th Ill. Inf.
Lynch, Edwin, Asst. Surg. 6th N. Y. Inf.
Lecky, W. K., Private, Co. H, 11th Ill. Inf.
Lee, George W., Sergt. Co' B, 152d Ill. Inf.
Manix, Luke, Private Co. D, 19th Ill. Inf.
Mayo, Henry, Corp. Co. I, 11th Ill. Inf.
McDonald, R. D., Co. B, 96th Ohio Inf.
McKinley, L. L., Private, Cogswell's Battery.
McMullen, C. W., Private Co. E, 31st Ill. Inf.
Mahar, Jerry, Private Co. A, 64th Ill. Inf.
McLaughlin, Charles, Private Co. F, 15th Ill. Inf.

(Seth C. Earl Post Ottawa, Illinois, Continued.)

Nattinger, E. A., Private Co. C, 14th Ill. Cav.
Olds, J. E., Private Co. B, 52d Ill. Inf.
Parker, W. P., First Lieut. Co. II, 11th N. II. Inf.
Pierce, J. P., Private Co. G, 117th Ohio Inf.
Pettit, Charles E, Private Co. O, 111st Ill. Inf.
Pettit, J. W., Private Co. K., 142d Ill. Inf.
Phillemore, Wm., Private Co. C, 53d Ill. Inf.
Porter, S. W., Sergt. Major, 15th Ill. Cav.
Porter, S. F., Private Co. C, 1st Ill. Art.
Poundstone, Richard, Private Co. L, 15th Ill. Cav.   .
Pichard, W. E., Private Co. I, 2d Ohio, Heavy Art.   .
Phillips, C. D., Private Co. II, 57th Ill. Inf.
Peekham, G. E., Musician, 5th Wis. Inf.
Rambler, John J., Private Co. II, 54th Ill. Inf.
Raymond Wm., Drummer Co. A, 104th Ill. Inf.
Reese, C. M., Private Co. I, 24th Ill. Inf.
Rinker, Jacob, Private Co. K, 103d Ill. Inf.
Rising, James G., Private Co. K, 10th N. Y. Art.
Rising, L. A., Capt. Co. A, 10th N. Y. Art.
Roberts Edward H. Private Co. D, 20th Ohio Inf.
Roberts, Daniel W., Private Co. D 20th Ohio Inf.
Roberts, G. H., Private Co. G, 96th Ohio Inf.
Rood, H. A., Private Co G, 104th Ill. Inf.
Sapp, F. M., Capt. Co. K, 104th Ill. Inf.
Schindler, George, Private Co. D, 138th Ill. Inf.
Scisco, Orlando, private Cogswell's Battery.
Shaw, C. M., Private Co. I, 11th Ill. Inf.
Slager, E. S., Sergt. Co. C, 53d Ill. Inf.

(90th G. Earl Post, Ottawa, Illinois, Continued.)

Singer, W. P., Lieut. Co. K, 31st Mo. Inf.
Smith, Augustus, Private Co. B, 2d Ohio Art.
Smith, Chas. E., Private Co. A, 64th Ill. Inf.
Smith, Wm. H., Private Co. E, 101th Ill. Inf.
Snow, D. B., Co. K, 83d Ohio Inf.
Stewart, W. K., Private Co. K, 11th Ill. Inf.
Strait, E. H., Private Co. F, 36th Ill. Inf.
Stumph, Elisha H, Major, 53d Ill. Inf.
Talbot, Philander, Lieut. Co. B, 104th Ill. Inf.
Trask R. H., Private Co. A, 104th N. Y. Inf.
Troescher, Charles F, Private Co. E, Ringold's Battery.
Thomas, J. W., Private Co. E, 50th Ill. Inf.
Warner, Joel F., Private Co. F, 25th Mich. Inf.
Warner, J. I., Corp. Co. A, 153d Ill. Inf.
Warren, L. C., Private Cogswell's Battery.
Warriner, A. C., Private Co. B, 72d Ill. Inf.
Watson, J. H., Private Co. F, 76th Ohio Inf.
Weaver, L. E., First Lieut. Co. M, 12th Tenn. Cav.
Whipple, F. H., Major, 11th Ill. Inf.
Widmer, John H, Major, 10th Ill. Inf.
Willis, S. S., Private Co. L, 15th Ill. Cav.
Woodward, Royal S., Sergt. Co. G, 3d Wis. Inf.
Wyman, Peter, Private Co. I, 11th Ill. Inf.
Zeller, Jacob, Musician, 53d Ill. Inf.

RICHARD YATES,
The War Governor of Illinois.

Officers, Past Presidents and Members of

Seth C Earl W. R. C. No. 166,

OTTAWA, ILLINOIS.

OFFICERS.

Mrs. Mary A. Sapp.........................President
Mrs. Jennie D. McDonald......Senior Vice-President
Mrs. Susan S. Gibson....,.....Junior Vice-President
Mrs. Mary E. Warner ....Secretary
Mrs. Alice E. Stiefel......................Treasurer
Mrs. Susie S. Snow.........................Chaplain
Mrs. Josephine B. Rose ....Conductor
Mrs. Hannah Horan..........................Guard
Mrs. Emily A. Parrott..............Asst. Conductor
Mrs. Margaret E. Corcoran.............Asst. Guard

ORGANIST.

Mrs. Mina Hossack.   Mrs. Anna M. Olmstead, Asst.

COLOR BEARERS.

Mrs. Anna M. Prieseler.   Mrs. Matilda Vogel.
Mrs. Hattie Garden.   Mrs. Ida M. Brewer.

PAST PRESIDENTS.

Mrs. Ella T. Hapeman.   Mrs. Olive S. Rising.
Mrs. Susia A. Dyer.   Mrs. Emoline M. Duffy

MEMBERS.

Mrs. Lurancie A. Clark.
Mrs. Maria M. Clairmont.
Mrs. Fannie King.
Mrs. Rachel J. Beckwith.
Mrs. Frances J. Beach.
Mrs. Roselia A. Vincent.
Mrs. Frank W. Talbot.
Mrs. Viney B. Fullerton.
Mrs. Elizabeth Hughes.
Mrs. Belle Bathurst.
Mrs. Ella J. Knapp.
Mrs. Mary E. Funk.
Mrs. Mary R. Campbell.
Mrs. Sarah A. Stumph.
Mrs. Lou D. Merrifield.
Mrs. Bertha Hetzner.
Mrs. Christian Vey.
Mrs. Mary D. Moody.
Mrs. Mary Lewis.
Mrs. Emma Holmes.
Mrs. Mary D. Bowman.
Mrs. Emeline M. Duffy.
Mrs. Anna Porter.
Mrs. Annie Eastabrook.
Mrs. Hannah Doran.
Mrs. Julia Wilhelm.
Mrs. Elizabeth Foley.
Mrs. Susie S. Snow.
Mrs. Anna B. Olmstead.
Mrs. Jane E. Weber.
Mrs. Emma W. Griffith.
Mrs. Mary E. Thompson.
Mrs. Rachel J. Beckwith.
Mrs. Edna Moore.
Mrs. Relefe Verner.
Mrs. Sarah E. Yockey.
Mrs. Anna Cole.
Mrs. Mary Ebersol.
Mrs. Clara Harper.
Mrs. Sarah J. Stumph.
Mrs. Barbara Hoffman.
Mrs. Winifred Moore.
Mrs. Mary Ringer.
Mrs. Helen C. Cooper.
Mrs. Josephine Keith.
Miss Mamie Fox.
Mrs. Malinda Parker.
Mrs. Emily A. Parrott.
Mrs. Adelia Ward.
Mrs. Lena M. Walters.
Mrs. Helen B. Weeks.
Mrs. Mary E. Pickens.
Mrs. Mary L. Pettit.

Mrs. Olive S. Rising.
Mrs. Nellie Brothers.
Mrs. Visa O. Morrill.
Mrs. Mary E. Berndt.
Mrs. Lucie S. Mechem.
Mrs. Ellen G. Hatheway.
Mrs. Helen M. Anthony.
Mrs. Rebecca Butterfield.
Mrs. Natilda E. Nattinger.
Mrs. Frederika Gleim.
Mrs. Madge G. Cooke.
Mrs. Jessie Robinson.
Mrs. Lizzie Farnsworth.
Mrs. Josephine A. Parr.
Mrs. Julia B. Richolson.
Mrs. Stella Hood.
Mrs. Marie E. Martin.
Mrs. Martha E. Mills.
Mrs. Hattie F. Olmstead.
Mrs. Georgia Perkins.
Miss Mary S. Poundstone.
Mrs. Georgia G. Cook.
Mrs. Margrettie Richardson
Mrs. Emily McDermott.
Mrs. Rhoda McDowell.
Mrs. Hattie E. Stevenson.
Mrs. Anna Priseler.
Mrs. Cordelia M. Hatheway.
Mrs. Margaret E. Corcoran.
Mrs. Fidealia Baker.
Mrs. Jane M. Rugg.
Mrs. Margaret A. Stumph.
Mrs. Daisy G. Muir.
Mrs. Olive Gay.
Miss Dorothy Lange.
Mrs. Addie B. Roberts.
Mrs. Catherine Humbert.
Mrs. Josephine Thorn.
Mrs. Hattie Garden.
Mrs. Sophronia Widmer.
Mrs. Helen E. Trask.
Mrs. Matilda Vogle.
Mrs. Eva L. Werner.
Miss Maud Fellows.
Miss Isabel Wallace.
Mrs. Ella T. Hapeman.
Mrs. Margaret Egan.
Mrs. Susan S. Gibson.
Mrs. Eleanor Hickling,
Mrs. Catherine Salisbury.
Mrs. Mary J. Johnson.
Mrs. Ida M. Brower.
Mrs. Mabel A. Moulton.

(Both C. Earl W. R. C Ottawa, Illinois, Continued.)

Mrs. Bertha R. Wolf.   Mrs. Sarah E. Pratt.
Mrs. Susan Singer.   Mrs. Anna Lindstrom.
Mrs. Blanche Strasser.   Mrs. Arietta Hall.
Mrs. Elizabeth Collis.   Mrs. Mina Hossack.
Mrs. Margaret Hager.   Mrs. Eliz'beth Bowermaster
Mrs. Ellen Lee.   Mrs. Ella Eichelberger.
Mrs. Laura D. Manchester. Mrs. Bertha M. Christmann
Mrs. Lou D. Merrifield.   Mrs. Josephine B. Rose.
Mrs. Harriet Egan.   Mrs. Lois M. Watson.
Mrs. Anna Herbster.   Mrs. Ella Weaver.
Miss Mae McDougall.   Mrs. Hannah Millard.
Mrs. Lizzie Keim.   Mrs. Jennie D. McDonald
Mrs. Sara M. Combs. ,   Mrs. Susan Cooley.
Mrs. Lizzie James.   Mrs. Annie Ayers.
Mrs. Sarah Cannon.   Miss Emma Watts.
Mrs. E. Louise Leland.   Mrs. Ella W. Hoffman.
Mrs. Minnie E. Mohr.   Mrs. Hattie Prichard.
Mrs. Sarah A. Olds.

Union Veterans Union,

OTTAWA, ILLINOIS.

Price Bros. Command.

Organized May 5th 1897.

OFFICERS.

D. A. NICHOLSON.............................Colonel
JOSEPH RIFORD.................Lieutenant-Colonel
M. HANIFEN.............................Adjutant

MEMBERS.

Armstrong, W. S., Co. II., 11th Ill. Inf.
Ayers, Oscar, Henshaw's Battery.
Burgess, Wm., Cogswell's Battery.
Bailey, Mathew, Co. K, 8th Ill. Cav.
Brady, W. I., Co. B, 76th Pa. Inf.
Clairmont, Lewis, Co. D, 88th Ill. Inf.
Crawford, Martin, Co. I 4th Ill. Cav.
Combs, J. R., Co. D, 127th Ill. Inf.
Collamore, Wm. Co. G, 58 Ill. Inf.
Channel, J. Co. E, 3rd Ill. Cav.
Dilley, Leonard, Co. G, 1st W. Va. Inf.
Flanagan, Thomas, Co. A, 1st Wis. Cav.
Graham, John, Co. B, 1st Ill. Lt. Art.
Grant, O. B., Co. C, 53rd Ill. Inf.
Hanifen, M., Co. B, 1st N. J. Art,
Harner. J. W., Co. C, 53rd Ill. Inf.
Harner, David, Co. I, 53rd Ill. Inf.
Hamilton, Wm., Co. C, 1st Ill. Art.
Jencks, William, Co. K, 129th Ill. Inf.
Jones, W. M., Co. G, 104th Ill.
Jaka, John, Co. I, 9th Ill. Inf.
Keim, Martin, Co, I, 24th Ill. Inf.
Martin, Benj., Co. G, 2nd Vt. Inf.
McKinley, Leroy L., Cogswell's Battery.
Morrisey, Lawrence, Co. II, 90th Ill. Inf.
Nicholson, D. A., Co. K, 39th Ill. Inf.
Porter, S. F., Co. C., 1st Ill. Art.
Riford, Joseph, Co. K., 31st Wis. Inf.
Singer, E. S., Co. C., 53rd Ill. Inf.
Schlosser, Christian, Co. I, 2nd Wis. Inf.
Smith, John, Co. E. 127th Ill. Inf.
Singer, W. P., Co. K., 31st Mo. Inf.
Wilhelm, August, Co. M., 7th Ill. Cav.

Maj.-Gen. Nelson A. Miles.

Officers and Members of

Co. C, 3d Illinois Vol. Inf.

Organized at Ottawa, Illinois, August 7th, 1877.

Mustered into the U. S. Vol. service May 7th, 1898, at Springfield. Mustered out January 19th, 1899, at Ottawa, Ill. Spanish-American war.

COMMISSIONED OFFICERS.

Sidney R. Blanchard..........................Captain
Harry H. Harden.....................1st Lieutenant
Chas. L. Gapen............ ....2d Lieutenant

NON-COMMISSIONED OFFICERS.

S. D. Colwell.............................1st Sergeant
E. R. Witte ....Q. M. Sergeant
F. T. Baker...................................Sergeant
D. W. Gregg..................................Sergeant
F. H. Wilson.................................Sergeant
F. A. Jordan................................Sergeant
I. R. Campbell, (deceased)...................Corporal
A. M. Bailey ....Corporal
L. M. Hoffman........ ....Corporal
B. S. Jordan.......................... ......Corporal
C. M. Butters..... ....Corporal
F. A. Sapp...................................Corporal
L. R. Huston.............................Corporal
Fred Peck ....Corporal
Sam'l Pearson..............................Corporal
A. M. Chamberlain.......... ....Musician
G. E. Vincent, (deceased)..................Musician

PRIVATES.

Anderson, C. A.
Anderson, J. F.
Antrim, A. K.
Barnard, S.
Bee, A. W.
Berge, B. O.
Boyd, R.
Bruck, O. J.
Burnett, Jno.
Campbell, H. H.
Compton, Jno.
Cosgrove, Jos.
Cosgrove, Wm.
Dwyer, J. J.
Edgcomb, Benj.
Erdman, A.
Fey, Carl
Flynn, J. L.
Forster, C. S.
Gavin, M. J.
Gedney, R.
Gleim, W. S.
Gosney, F.
Green, Jno. H.
Hayden, J. F.
Himes, Edw.
Hoffman, A. C.
Hollands, —.
Horan, F. E.
Houston, E.
Hupp, C. W.
Hawse, Robt. M.
Iliff, R. C.
Jaka, O. R.
Jaka, W. J.
Jencks, W. E.
Johnson, C. E.
Kelly, T. F.
Klaus, Philip
*Krause, W. H.
Krouse, B.
Lehman, E. O.
Lehman, L. H
*Leland, R. M.
Le Rette, Fred,
Le Rette, H. W.

Lewis, J. W.
Lloyd, E.
Lock, C. E.
Looney, P. J.
Lunney, J. H.
MacKinlay, W. E.
Maher, C.
Maierhofer, C. E.
Mann, C. L.
Marland, J. R.
Marsh, C. C.
Mayo, R.
*McCoy, Albert
McKinney, D. M.
McLaughlin, A.
McMichael, F. F.
Meehan, B. J.
Meyers, G. T.
Mitchell, J. E.
Moloney, F.
Monogue, J.
Nicholson, J. M.
*Osmunson, M. E.
*Osmunson, O. O.
Peck, C. O.
Phelan, T. F.
Pike, W. A.
Raley, C. I.
Raymond, Roy
Reynolds, H. J.
Russell, A. H.
Scott, F. C.
*Shuler, E. O.
Smith, A. E.
Smith, F. A.
*Smith, J. A.
Strohmeyer, R.
Walley, C. A.
Weaver, J. H.
Weger, H. G.
Widmer, F. W.
Wilhelm, F. A.
Wilhelm, W. W.
Wilson, T. C.
Windle, T. E.
Witt, F. H.
Wyman, G. H.

*Deceased.

Union Soldiers Now Living at
Ottawa, Illinois,

Not Members of the Local G. A. R. Post.

Martin Baker, private Co. K, 11th Ill. Inf.
J. B. Baumgardner, private Co. E. 101th Ill. Inf.
P. G. Boers, private Henshaw's Battery.
F. M. Belrose, private Co. B, 18th Pa. Inf.
C. H. Belrose, private Co. C, 44th Ill. Inf.
Alvin Chapin, Co. B, 4th Ill. Cav.
W. G. Cunningham, Cogswells Battery.
William Deukart, Co. E, 104th Ill.
Julius Emerick, Co. A, 64th Ill.
M. Flamm, Co. A, 86th Ill.
A. J. Gabler, Co. G, 1st Mass. Cav.
E. H. Hollis, Co. A. 104th Ill.
Thos. Larkin, Lt. Co. K, 90th Ill.
John N. Lee, Co. D, 10th N. Y. Hvy. Art.
Daniel Mason, Co. G, 104th Ill.
J. D. McDowell, Co. A, 66th Ill.
S. E. Pearson, Co. E, 3rd Ohio Cav.
Patrick Rafferty, Cogswell's Battery.
C. W. Reynolds, Co. C, 1st Ill. Art.
C. H. Stockley, Co. G, 121st N. Y.
T. O. Sullivan, Co. A., U. S. Engineers.
W. H. Sunderland, Co. F, 16th N. Y. Cav.
Robert Wallace, Co. C, 7th Ill. Cav.
C. E. Wing, Co. E, 53rd Ill. Inf.
J. Blodgett, Sergt. Co. L, 2nd Mich. Cav.
L. M. Chamberlain, Co. —, 31st Wis.
J. R. Cross, Co. B, 72nd Ill.
T. J. Carew, Co. A, 5th Conn.

J. H. Drake, Co. C, 53rd Ill. Inf.
Thomas Forbes, Co. K, 138th Ill.
Lewis Grover, Co.   , 7th Ill. Cav.
Loomfield Green, Co   , 104th Ill.
H. A. Johnson, Co. A, 57th Mass.
E. B. Lovejoy, Co. D, 13th N. H. Inf.
Chas. McNanna, Co. E, 191st Ohio.
John Fribbs, Cogswell's Battery.
James McKul, Co.   , 23d Ill. Inf.
Edward Mooney, Co. A, 38th Ill. Inf.
A. H. Mariefield.
Frank Pickins, Sergt. Co. A, 104th Ill.
J. W. Sherman, Co. A, 108th Ill.
Ralph Sanderson, Co. K, 53rd Ill.
Henry Wyman, Co. A, 53rd Ill.
James Timmons, Co. I, 52nd Ill.
J. P. Wilson, Co. L, 15th Ill. Cav.
George Colwell, Co. K, 138th Ill.
O. W. Green, Co. E, 26th Ill.
George W. Whaley, Co. K, 129th Ill.
John Viehman, Co. E, 27th Pa. Inf.
David Larriaux, Co. B. 78th Ill.
H. O. Shaver, Co. C, 20th Mich Inf.
D. B. Himenover, Co. I, 53rd Ill.

Mexican War Soldiers now Living at Ottawa, Illinois.

John F. Gibson, Co. G, 1st Ill. Inf.
W. P. Gregg, Co. E, 1st Ill. Inf.
Fred W. Mangas, Co. K, 1st U. S. Art.
Wm. Osman, Q. M. Sergt. 1st Ill. Inf.

Gen. Judson C. Kilpatrick.

JOHN BROWN.

STREATOR.

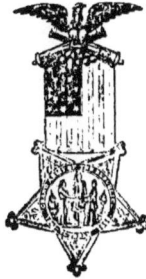

Officers, Past Post Commanders and Members of

Streator Post, No. 68, G. A. R.

STREATOR, ILL.

OFFICERS.

A. S. Ross.................................Commander
GEO. B. RAND.... ....S. V. Commander
N. J. HORNBECK........... ......J. V. Commander
J. J. TAYLOR ....Surgeon
J. C. HUNTER.............................Chaplain
E. S. CARR .... - ...,Adjutant
J. S. RYON..........................Quartermaster
GEO. H. DUNN ....Officer of the Day
HENRY STUDEBAKER...........Officer of the Guard
THOS. J. RUNKER.. ....Sergeant Major
DAVID C. GALLOWAY........Quartermaster Sergeant

PAST POST COMMANDERS.

W. W. BEAN,   J. T. MURDOCK,
ISAAC KEAR,   J. S. RYON,
A. B. PAULEY,   S. B. PATCH,
S. MCFEELY,   J. C. HUNTER,

MEMBERS.

Allen, William, private, Co. H, 77th Ill. Inf., miner.

Ammons, I. H., private Henshaw's Battery, mason.

Argubright, Caleb, private Co. C, 139th Ill. Inf., farmer.

Artus, Reese, private Co. E, 97th Pa. Inf., janitor.

Beau, W. W., private Co. A, 16th N. Y. Inf., printer.

Barrickman, M. J., private Co. D, 20th Ill. Inf., mine operator.

Burson, M. L., private Co. H, 40th Ind. Inf., physician.

Billingsley, Geo., private Co. G, 4th Iowa Cav., dray man.

Boyd, Jacob, private Battery D, 1st Ill. Art., laborer.

Birt, Geo. E, private Co. E, 77th Ind. Inf., carpenter.

Brewer, Geo. W., private Co. D, 77th Ill. Inf., engineer.

Bell, Joe, private Co. D, 63rd Ohio Inf., clergyman.

Blakemore, John,

Barr, P. F., private Co. D, 33rd Iowa Inf., civil engineer.

Brown, Wm., private Co. F, 104th Ill. Inf., farmer.

Birtwell, Robert, private Co. F, 104th Ill. Inf., farmer.

Carr, E. J., private Co. C, 146th Ill. Inf., merchant.

Cooper, William, private Co. G, 104th Ill. Ipf., farmer.

Coe, John, private Co. G, 18th Pa. Cav., farmer.

Cutler, Geo., private Co. F, 21st Ill. Inf., merchant.

Comfort, Patrick, private Co. G, 1st U. S. Engineers, miner.

Clay, James, private Vaughn's Ind. Battery, farmer.

Carey, John, private Co. B, 57th Ill. Inf., farmer.

Carrington, James, private Co. F, 33rd Ill. Inf., laborer.

Courtney, John C., private Co. I, 53rd Ill. Inf., wagon maker.

Callihan, Chas. A., sergt., Co. E, 7th W. Va. Inf., miner.

Campbell, John H., private Co. G, 104th Ill. Inf., carpenter.

Cooper, John, private Co. I, 32nd Ill. Inf., farmer.

Dunn, Geo. H., private Co. G, 26th Mich. Inf. barber.

Daugherty, F. M., sergt. Co. F, 104th Ill. Inf., farmer.

Donaldson, Thomas, private Co. I, 32nd Ill. Inf., farmer.

Eastwood, A. J., private Co. G, 104th Ill. Inf., carpenter.

Flannigan, Thomas, private Co. K, 129th Ill. Inf., teamster.

Ford, John I., private Co. D, 104th Ill. Inf., mail carrier.

Fleck, Michael, private Co. D, 53rd Ill. Inf., farmer.

Fletcher, R. D., private Co. F, 122nd Ill. Inf., supt. of mines.

Flood, James, private Co. C, 53rd Ill. Inf., miner.

Felger, John, 2nd Lt., Co. H, 77th Ill. Inf., insurance agent.

Funk, David A., private Co. G, 63rd Ill. Inf., laborer.

(Streator Post, No. 68, Continued.)

Galloway, David C., private Co. E, 139th Ind. Inf., carpenter.
Glassar, Fred, private Co. I, 24th Ill. Inf., miner.
Gaut, Geo., private Co. C, 11th Ill. Inf., constable.
Griffith, John, private Co. E, Ind. Batt. and Pa. Art., miner.
Gelson, Chas., private Co. I, 55th Mass. Inf., miner.
Hornbeck, N. J., private Co. E, 104th Ill. Inf., contractor.
Hunter, J. C., private Co. C, 64th Ill. Inf., mail carrier.
Hunt, Lovejoy, private Co. D, 20th Ill. Inf., farmer.
Hubbard, F. D., private Co. D, 6th Wis. Inf., blacksmith.
Hoessel, Jno. A., private Co. B, 77th Ill. Inf., cabinet maker.
Hudson, Geo., private Co. I, 11th Ill. Inf., farmer.
Hood, Thos. G., private Co. A, 98th Ohio Inf., clay manufacturer.
Hill, W. C., private Co. H, 20th Ill. Inf., florist.
Howe, L. D., Mus. Co. I, 15th Ill. Inf., supt.
Hiner, Jno. D., private 163rd Pa. Inf., brick maker.
Hall, Robert, private Co. C, 2nd Iowa Inf., livery man.
Howarth, Geo., private Co. K, 31st Ill. Inf., miner.
Hopple, Peter, Mus., Co. H, 104th Ill. Inf., farmer.
Harber, John D., private Co. D, 129th Ill. Inf., farmer.
Jardine, Duncan, private Co. D, 1st Mich. Inf., miner.
Kear, Isaac, private Co. E, 4th N. Y. Cav., miner.
Krimshaw, M.
Kelley, Wm. A., private Co. A, 53rd Ill. Inf., meat market.
Kenna, John, private Co. C, 120th Ill. Inf., miner.
Lyons, John, Sergt. Co. G, 17th Ill. Inf., blacksmith.
Longton, John, Mus. Co. K, 129th Ill. Inf., blacksmith.
Ley, Wm. L., private Co. H, 86th Ill. Inf., plasterer.
Merritt, Mallory, private Co I, 104th Ill. Inf., laborer.
Mills, L. C., private Co. C, 44th Ill. Inf., weighmaster.
Morell, Mathew, private Co. A, 96th Pa. Inf., miner.
Morse, Orrin, private Co. A, 125th Ohio Inf., miner.
Murdock, J. T., private Co. B, 3rd Mo. Cav., lawyer.
Morse, Chas. W., private Co. K, 1st Ill. Lt. Art., engineer.
Mowbray, Thos., Henshaw's Battery, miner.
Mackey, Chas., private Co. F, 104th Ill. Inf., merchant.
Massey, Jesse, private Co. A, 129th Ill. Inf., miner.
Mackey, Geo. W., private Co. F, 104th Ill. Inf. farmer.
Murray, Thos. L., private Co. E, 33rd Ill. Inf., teamster.
McFeely, S., Sergt. Co. K, 39th Mass. Inf., lumber dealer.
McLana, Daniel, private Co. E, 129th Ill. Inf., janitor.
McMastus, John.
McQuown, Sherman, private Co. A, 129th Ill. Inf., carpenter.

McQuown, William, private Co. E, 26th Ill. Inf., farmer.

McFadden, John W., private Co. C, 152nd Ill. Inf., R. R. P. O. clerk.

McMastus, Basil, private Co. H. 4th Ind. Cav., miner.

Noel, William, private Co. C, 76th Ill. Inf., miner.

Painter, A. J., private Co. A, 53rd Ill. Inf., farmer.

Plumb, Ralph, Capt. U. S. Vol., financier.

Plimmer, John, private Co. I, 27th Pa. Inf., janitor.

Paumb, John B., musician, Co. D, 18th Iowa Inf., brick manufacturer.

Pauley, A. B., private Co. H, 11th Ill. Inf., harness maker.

Phibbs, Thomas M., private Co. K, 4th Iowa Cav., laborer.

Payne, Lemuel, private Co. K, 93rd Ill. Inf., laborer.

Painter, U. S, private Co. I, 15th Ill. Cav., farmer.

Patch, S. B., private Co. K, 136th Pa. Inf., foundry.

Patton, David A., private Co. E, 129th Ill. Inf., farmer.

Ross, A. S., private Co. I, 110th Ill. Inf., watchman.

Rand, Geo. B., private Co. L, 1st Vermont Cav., R. R. conductor.

Ryon, J. S., private Co. K, 75th Ill. Inf., justice of the peace.

Rankin, Thomas J., private Co. D, 85th Pa. Inf., teacher.

Richards, Henry, private Co. E, 12th Ill. Cav., engineer.

Rush, Nicholas, private Co. F, 104th Ill. Inf., farmer.

Riel, Paul, private Co. E, 9th Wis. Inf., drayman.

Rathbun, E. R., private Co. H., 11th Ill. Inf., invalid.

Studebaker, Henry, private Co. D, 81st Ill. Inf., farmer.

Shearer, F. S., private Co. G, 86th Ill. Inf., carpenter.

Spendlove, Edward, private Co. A, 3rd Ill. Cav., laborer.

Spears, A. J., private Co. C, 57th Ind. Inf., blacksmith.

Shay, John H., private Co. F, 104th Ill. Inf., lawyer.

Stormer, John, private Co. I, 47th Ill. Inf., blacksmith.

Seddard, Wm., private Co. D, 21st Pa. Inf., miner.

Showman, Henry P., private Co. I, 104th Ill. Inf., retired.

Taylor, John J., private Co. K, 20th Ill Inf., physician.

Taylor, Geo., private Co. D, 104th Ill. Inf., teamster.

Tidaback, John, private Battery D, 5th Wis. Art. miner.

Trout, Alex., private Co. D., 125th Pa. Inf., tailor.

Ward, J. G., private Co. H. 126th Ill. Inf., miner.

White Dennis, private Co. K, 100th Ill. Inf., barber.

Worrell, H. N., private Co. A, 53rd Ill. Inf., miner.

Wells, Lewis C., private Co. H, 104th Ill. Inf., farmer.

Worrell, W. H. private Co. I, 5th W. Va. Cav., laborer,

Woolford, Josiah, private Co. I, 67th Pa. Inf., miner.

1912818

Officers, Past Presidents and Members of

Streator W. R. C., No. 116,

STREATOR, ILL.

Organized in 1888.

OFFICERS.

Ida E. Hunter.... ....President
Larah A. Larkin........ ....S. V. President
Mary A. Kear.......................J. V. President
Sarah E. Painter..... ....Secretary
Sara E. Dicus.... ....Treasurer
Aurelia Billingsley........................Chaplain
Lottie Glover...........................Conductor
Mary E. Lambert.............................Guard
Bertha Sullivan...... ....Assistant Conductor
Estella Butcher................... ..Assistant Guard .
Maggie Mowbray....` ....1st Color Bearer
Carrie Eastwood...................2nd Color Bearer

PAST PRESIDENTS.

Martha Bean,	Mrs. Sarah Hall,
Mrs. Minnie Murdock,	Mrs. Ida Hunter,
Miss Emma Dagon,	Mrs. Bacon,
Miss Agnes Hall.	Mrs. Sarah Painter,
Mrs. Jessie Merritt,	Mrs. Margaret A. Ross.

PAST DEPARTMENT SENIOR VICE PRESI-
DENT.

Mrs. Margaret A. Ross.

MEMBERS.

Atkins, Esther
Augubright, Sarah
Anderson, Anna
Alderson, Mrs.
Bean, Martha
Beeth, Dezeria
Birt, Clara
Butcher, Estella
Burson, Mary
Billingsley, Aurelia
Boyd, Mary
Carpenter, Lulu
Carr, Josie
Crampton, Mrs.
Denaple, Mary
Dove, Mrs.
Dicus, Sara
Dowling, Mary
Dixon, Drusilla
Eastwood, Carrie
Eddy, Jane
Flick, Pauline
Finkler, M. E.
Flannigan, Sarah
Gaut, Flora
Gridley, Hester
Glover, Lottie
Gudgel, Mrs.
Godfrey, Mrs.
Griffith, Jessie
Hall, Agnes
Hall, Sarah
Hodson, Mary E.
Harding, Mrs.
Hicks, Mrs.
Hunter, Ida E.
Hoopes, Hattie
Hazel, Mary
Howe, Marian
Jones, Rachel
Johnson, Cora
Kear, Mary
Kelly, Caroline
Krouse, Bertie
Lambert, Mary
Leek, Sarah

Larkin, Sarah
Lobb, Martha
Longdo, Mrs.
Morse, Amelia
Mowbray, Maggie
Mills, Lou
Murdock, Minnie
Mohler, Nancy
Murray, Rebecca
Muckey, Harriet
Miles, Lizzie
Meyers, Charlotte
McGuown, Anna
McBane, Anna
McFeely, Mrs.
McDermott, Mrs.
Nelson, Sarah
Osborn, Sarah
Prafcke, Gertrude
Pauley, A. B.
Patch, Sarah
Patch, Sadie
Phillips, Lucretia
Painter, Amanda
Painter, Sarah
Perry, Sarah
Painter, Anna
Plimmer, Mary
Ryon, Julia
Rathbun, Clara
Ross, Margaret A.
Ross, Pearl G.
Rich, Olive
Rand, Mary
Rainey, Mrs.
Snyder, Sarah
Sharlol, Mrs.
Sweetser, Mrs.
Saddal, Mary
Skinner, Mrs.
Sullivan, Bertha
* Spears, Sarah
White, Esther
Warren, Cathrine
Weller, Mary E.
Wilkes, Mrs.

Weller, Mrs.

U. S. Battleship Maine.

Officers and Members of

Co. A, 3rd Ill. Vol. Inf.

Organized at Streator, Ill., Aug. 22, 1875. Mustered into the U. S. service May 10, 1898. Mustered out January, 1899. Spanish-American War.

COMMISSIONED OFFICERS.

Wm. H. Higby................................Captain
Charles P. Gaut................1st Lieutenant
Benj. R Hall.......................2nd Lieutenant

NON-COMMISSIONED OFFICERS.

F. B. Killifer................................1st Sergeant
Frank Sipe............................Q. M. Sergeant
Ross Sipe....................................Sergeant
Roy E. Stiles................................Sergeant
H. P. Trout..................................Sergeant
F. H. Buzzicot, (Chicago)...............Sergeant
Wm. Hennessey...........................Corporal
Lewis Graves...............................Corporal
Fred Gaut...................................Corporal
M. O. Leech................................Corporal
Chas. Edwards............................Corporal
J. B. McCune (Morrison).............Corporal
L. B. Bradisa...............................Corporal
Frank Barrickman.......................Corporal
Wm. Holcomb.............................Corporal
W. T. Wright..............................Corporal
W. F. Wilkinson.........................Corporal
C. W. Walker.............................Corporal
Albert W. Lakin.........................Musician
J. O. Stewart.............................Musician
E. M. Buel, (Chicago).................Artificer
Wm. Mitchell..............................Wagoner

PRIVATES.

Aker, Walter M.

Baldwin, L. M.

Barker, O. M., Peoria.

Barnhart, J., Dwight.

Bever, S. D.

Breckenridge, J. C.

Bruce, J., Ransom.

Clark, Geo. W.

Cox, Merril M.

Davidson, Sidney E.

Dixon, Wm.

Dobbs, Rob E., Ky.

Donahue, M. J.

Elliott, Geo. T.

Euteneuer, S.

Ferguson, James

Follmer, W. M., Chi.

Fout, Wm. Manville.

Fox, D. S., Dwight.

Geis, W. C., Dwight.

Giles, Rollin

Gipe, C. R., Rockford.

Gould' C. C., Dwight.

Groshans, Jacob

Gurke, Herman, Chi.

Hall, J. H., Wenona.

Hasara, Geo., Rangley.

Haupt, A., Chicago,

Hearing, C. H., Dwight,

Hill, Clark

Hill, Ed. D.

Hix, Wm., Tampico.

Houshin, L., Cornell.

Irrgang. C. H.

Jensen, J. M., Dwight.

Jockisch, H., Chicago.

Johnson, Henry

Johnson, Howard

Klughart, M.

Libby, Harry

Lonnsberry, J. P.

Mann, C., Chicago.

Masters, Fremont

Meitzler, T. F. Chicago.

Michie, John

Miles, Hurley C.

Mortland, E., Misseal.

Muszynski, J., Chicago.

Norton, D. C., Joliet.

O'Brien, J. J.

Olmstead, Alonzo.

Olmstead, Elmer

Painter, Isaac

Peters, Claude

Potter, Stanley, Chi.

Pugh, Wm.

Ramsey, Hugh.

Rich, C. D.

Riss, Edward, Band.

Ryon, Wm.

Sauer, Wm., S. Chi.

Schneider, J., Dwight.

Shoeberlein, L., Band.

Skafgard, C., Dwight.

Slyder, F. Dwight.

Smith, Felix, Dwight.

Smith, Frank

Sokal, George.

Spaulding, H. S., Chi.

Spires, Frank

Springer, Guy

Springer, Robt.

Stevenson, T.

Uhrin, George

Walkowik, W., Chi.

Walters, W. S.

Wentland, R.

Waters, J. Dwight.

Watkins, W. B. Dwight.

Wentling, Peter, Mil.

Wheeler, J. W.

Williams, Walter

Weomer, Andrew,

IN
MEMORIAM.

Union Soldiers Buried in the Riverwood Cemetery Streator.

Warren Rockwood, F, 104th Illinois.
John Akhurst, C, 129th Illinois.
Edwin B. Washburn, 27th Illinois.
G. Cox, Captain A, 18th New York cavalry.
E. Edison, Co. and Regt. unknown.
Amos Hamilton, Co. and Regt. unknown.
Wm. Hodge, Co. and Regt. unknown.
—- Croege, Co. and Regt unknown.
Geo. W. Green, Co. and Regt. unknown.
John Liedke, Co. and Regt. unknown.
O. F. Bane, C, 8th Illinois.
A. Eckert, G, 129th Illinois.
William Pierson, Pennsylvania Regt.
Wm. H. Dagen, corporal K, 125th Regt. and 10th Indiana cavalry.
Chas Dagen, I, 43rd Ohio.
B. F. Dagen, K, 85th Ohio,
John F. Perkins, G, 17th Illinois.
Joseph Jackson, A, 41st. Ohio
John E. Williams, H, 11th Illinois cavalry.
Wm. H. Smith, D, 104th Ill.
Marlin C. Donagho, B, 85th Pennsylvania, died Oct. 25, 1881.
F. B. Darling, C, 7th Illinois, died Jan. 11, 1883.
John Morse, A, 128th Ohio.
G. W. Sidwell, A, 70th Ohio.
W. R. White, H, 138th Illinois.
T. W. Vineyard, B, 138th Illinois.

Henry H. Fusselman, captain, F, 19th Ohio.

W, Elliott, A, 10th Missouri.

H. L. Merritt, Henshaw's Battery.

C. E. Bale, H, 16th Iowa.

L. G. Egbert, captain, C, 59th Ohio.

B. F. Washburn, G, — New York.

John Honey, of the Navy.

John C. Campbell, E, 26th Illinois, March 30, 1890.

Chas. Prindle, C, 76th Illinois, April, 1890.

Luther Warren, I, 31st Illinois.

Christ Christfellow, D, 104th Ill.

Cassius M. Clark, A, 7th Indiana cavalry.

Freeman Bliss, D, 36th Illinois.

John Rockwood, F, 12th Illinois.

John B. Gregg, D, 91st Illinois, April 1890.

John H. Armstrong, H. 139th Ohio.

J. J. Johnson, I, 6th New York Heavy Artillery,

Geo. L. Richards, E, 89th Ill.

Christ Haney, A, 127th Illinois.

James Hall, E, 15th Ohio.

Porter Holcomb, I, 9th Michigan cavalry.

Harvey Kirkendall, F, 20th Illinois.

Joseph H. Taggart, F, 50th Ohio.

James Hill, B, 2nd Ohio Light artillery.

Oliver C. Bacon, 14th Ohio light artillery.

Wm. R. Snyder, sergeant, B, 129th Illinois.

C, W. Keller, 145th Pennsylvania.

George Wight, H, 16th New York.

Philip Thrull, I, 9th Michigan cavalry.

Frank Wantland, K, 119th Indiana.

Henry Beard, D, 91st Illinois.

John Wonders, G, 49th Pennsylvania.

James Edson, C, 48th Illinois.

William J. Kelly, Corporal Cogswell's Battery.

Clement Forney, (no record.)

Orson McIloy, C, 129th Illinois.

Wm. Patterson, Co. B, 1st N. Y. mounted rifles.

John McDermott, died May 20, 1899.

There are also two Streator boys who were in the Spanish-American war buried in Riverwood cemetery, Sergeant Frank Killifer. Co. A, 3d Illinois infantry.

Corporal Claude W. Peters, Co. A, 3d Illinois infantry.

WORKS AND OFFICE:

202, 204, 206, 208 Iowa Ave.

S. B. PATCH,

Manufacturer of all kinds of

Foundry and
Machine Work.

Architectural Iron and Steel.

Repairing and New Work.

Streator, - - Illinois.

PHILLIPS' CEMETERY.

Erastus J. Strange, 3d Illinois.
Franklin Hoobler, G, 129th Illinois.
John Bemerick, G, 129th Illinois.
Joel Wilmott, A, 129th Illinois.
James Houckins, F, 33d Illinois.
Willoughby Houckins, F, 135th Illinois.
Henry Houckins, G, 129th Illinois.
Wm. J. Warner, C, 14th Illinois.
Daniel Dougherty, F, 104th Illinois.
John Pope, Cogswell's battery.
William P. Moss, Co. and Regt. unknown.
Levi C. Hauger, K, 85th Pennsylvania.

BARNHART'S CEMETERY

John Sawyer, E, 104th Illinois.
James M. Mason, C, 26th Illinois.
A. M. Letz, C, 53rd Illinois.
H. J. Atwater, 39th Illinois.
Thomas Kelly, 53rd Illinois.
W. R. Reece, Co. C, 105th Ohio.
Hiram Helm, Co. and Regt. unknown.
Myron Kingsbury, Co. and Regt. unknown.
Robert Johnson.

MOON'S CEMETERY.

Henry Cox, Co. and Regt. unknown.
William Spicer, Co. and Regt. unknown.
Amos Mott, Co. and Regt. unknown.
Halsic Eltharpe, Co. and Regt. unknown.

CATHOLIC CEMETERY.

John Lawler, F, 5th Penn. Heavy Artillery.
Peter Balenciter, A, 44th Illinois.
Patrick Butterfield, of the Navy.
John Wilson, D, 19th Illinois.
John McDermott, F, 47th Illinois.

LOSTLANDS CEMETERY.

John Kennedy, 63rd Illinois.
Philip Campbed, 1st Illinois light artillery.

NARAMOUR'S CEMETERY.

George Connor, A. 129th Illinois.

MACKEY'S CEMETERY.

Mat. Morrison, C, 53rd Illinois.
Eli Gum, Co. and Regt. unknown.

Streator Zouaves---Champion Fancy Drill Team.

STREATOR, ILLINOIS.

OFFICERS.

W. B. Keller..................................Captain
A. J. Bevan............................1st Lieutenant
Fred Reinhard.........................2d Lieutenant
J. E. Russell...............................Sergeant

PRIVATES.

G. W. Bohnam,
J. I. Brannon,
J. H. Cook,
Wm. Carew,
B. Davenport,
Wm. Fox,
Ed. Grossman,
Chas. Glover,
I. T. Gaut,
Geo. Hardy,
F. W. Keller,
G. T. Knox,
Chas. Kruger,
Wm. Kruger,

O. Lorenz,
Geo. Lloyd,
Ira Messersmith,
J. B. Pickworth,
Jno. Patterson,
A. T. Poor,
Wm. Robb,
A. H. Raymond,
Jno. Reeder,
E. R. Schurman,
R. H. Schurman,
Wm. Sullivan,
Hiram Warren,
Wm. Welter,

Edward Zilm.

EX-MEMBERS.

Harry Barrackman,
Robt. Clendenen,
Albert Gurney,
Wm. Heineke,
W. H. Hornbeck,
Geo. Leonardy,

Wm. Pugh,
Lloyd Painter,
Frank Russell,
Wm. Stortz,
B. Tiffany,
Harry Trout.

J. C. Ames
Lumber Co.,

Dealers in

Sash,

Doors,

Mouldings,

Lime, Cement,

Patent Plaster.

BUILDING MATERIAL OF ALL KINDS.

Estimates Furnished.

Office Tel. 80.
Residence Tel. 2-58.

512 East Main Street,

STREATOR,   ILL.

104th Ill. Vol. Inf.

Organized at Ottawa, in August, 1862.

ROSTER OF THE SURVIVORS.

FIELD AND STAFF.

DOUGLAS HAPEMAN, Ottawa, Ill.
JOHN H. WIDMER, Ottawa, Ill.
JULIUS A. FREEMAN, Millington, Ill.

COMPANY A.

Arnold, Sidney V., Ipswich, S. Dak.
Baker, Nathaniel, Seneca, Ill.
Bush, John M., Sutton, Neb.
Cantlin, John A., Webster, Neb.
Daggett, Wm. H., Ottawa, Ill.
Ferguson, A. T., Kansas City, Mo.
Fuller, Charles, Graysville, or Ringgold, Ga.
Green, Bloomfield, Ottawa, Ill.
Hollis, E. H., Ottawa, Ill.
Horn, William, Ottawa, Ill.
Knapp, W. H., Ottawa, Ill.
Logan, J., Colby, Kan.
Norton, Wm. H., Earlville, Ill.
O'Reilly, Michael, 910 12th St. Chicago, Ill.
Prescott, Alphonso, Eldorado, Kan.
Pickens, Frank, Ottawa, Ill.
Raymond, Wm., Ottawa, Ill.
Redell, H., Kiowa, Barber Co., Kan.
Roach, James, Charlotte, Livingston Co., Ill.
Smith, Anton, Grand Ridge, Ill.
Stevenson, D. W., Streator, Ill.
Trobridge, E. J., 646 S. Spring St., Los Angeles Cal.
Varney, D., Kingman, Kan.
Warren, Lucian, Leland, Ill.
Weuve, Ulysses, State Center, Iowa.

(101 Illinois Vol. Inf. Continued.)

COMPANY B.

Angell, Benj. W., Lodemia, Livingston Co., Ill.
Asherman, Balser, Dewey, Champaign Co., Ill.
Barmore, Edward, Waukegan, Ill.
Barton, W. J., Walnut, Juniata Co., Pa.
Bradish, Chas. A. Ransom, Ill.
Burgess, Sid. W., Tonica, Ill.
Chace, Gardner I.., Fitzgerald, Ga.
Clark, W. H., Mound City, Kan.
Conroe. G. R., 143 Garfield Ave., Middletown.
Clark, J. A., St. Paul, Minn.
Dahl, Peterson, Granville,'Ill.
Delaney, Patrick, Dodge, Neb.
Dickson, John, Reading, Kan.
Dunham, Asa, Rutland, Ill.
Grist, O. E., Minneapolis, Ottawa Co. Kan.
Hall, Frank M., East Lynn, Ill.
Hall, Justin, S., Urbana, Ill.
Hall, W. S., 77 Ohio St., Chicago.
Howe, Geo. W. Tonica, Ill.
Hutchinson, Ed., Williamstown, Chickasaw Co., Ia.
Huling, Edward, Pontiac, Ill.
Johnson, Jacob, Hennepin, Ill.
Kinney, Herman L., Slayton, Minn.
McCormick, Nick., Utica, Ill.
Mellon, John M., Rockport, Kan.
Menz, Chas. W., Chatsworth, Ill.
Moos, Dominick, Nelson, Neb.
McCormick, James, Palisade, Neb.
Macson, Andrew, Pontiac, Ill.
Olson, Mons, Granville, Ill.
Patterson, S. H. Cornell, Ill.
Phelps, T, E. La Salle, Ill.
Redman, W. F. Wilson., Kan.
Richey, N., Redlands, Cal.
Robinson, A. Emington, Ill.
Robinson, A. G., Tonica, Ill.
Ross Grant, Souix City, Ia.
Ross, W. C., Blanchard or Shenandoah, Ia.
Sellars, G. W., Cadmus, Kan.
Stanford, David, Chatsworth, Ill.
Talbot, P., Ottawa, Ill.
Warnock, S. A., unknown.
West, Robert, Gilman, Ill.
Wheat, J. G., Mt. Vernon, Ia.
Woolley, Theron, unknown.
Woolstoncroft, J. P., Delight, Crawford Co., Ia.

(101 Illinois Vol. Inf. Continued.)

COMPANY C.

Avery, G. W., Fairfield, Neb.
Bankus, Henry D., Kansas City, Kan.
Bankus, Johnathan, Troy Grove, Ill.
Bankus, Samuel, Beloit, Kan.
Beck, H. E. Narka, Kan.
Bulliss, J. W., Iowa Falls, Ia.
Bulliss, Wm. T., Valentine, Neb.
Bunker, David, Haskell Inst., Lawrence Kan.
Clark, A. D., Atchison, Kan.
Cook, Almon L., Barreston, Neb.
Davis, J. M., Wellington, Kan.
Doane, Robt. C., Plainfield, Ill.
Edwards, Wm., Manchester, Kan.
Glover, F. L., Mound City, Kan.
Harris, Albert, 43 Washkenaw Ave., Chicago, Ill.
Harrold, Wm., Edinburg, Christian Co., Ill.
Hess, F. C., Ivester, Grundy Co., Ia.
Lewis, Joseph, Troy Grove, Ill.
Livers, John A., Mankato, Jewell Co., Kan.
Lynn, Samuel, Earlville, Ill.
Lyon, E. P., Williams, Ia.
McDowell, J. C., Meridan, Ill.
McSmith, Robert, Granville, Ill.
Mitchell, D. L., Columbus, O.
Moffitt. Geo. C., unknown.
Peters, Wm., Rockford, Ill.
Phillips, J., Broughton, Clay Co., Kan.
Ralph, James G., Aurora, Ill.
Ransberger, George, Troy Grove, Ill.
Rhoades, W. H. Anthony, Kan.
Risdon, Ambrose, Centralia, Nemaha Co., Kan.
Ralph, John B., Omaha, Neb.
Smiley, G. D., Grundy Center, Ia.
Stephens, E. L., Onawa, Monona Co., Ia.
Warner, John L., Streator, Ill.
Winslow, Wm. S., Earlville, Ill.
Wixom, C. J., Clay Center, Kan.
Winslow, L. W., Earlville, Ill.

COMPANY D.

Anderson, H. B., unknown.
Baker, Joseph, Ottawa, Ill.
Bramble, Alex., Goodland, Ind.
Bramble, James, Newmarket, Ia.
Brent, Robert S., Oconomowa, Wis.
Carmony, John. W., Endicott, Neb.
Clark, Grover C., Sterling, Ill.
Collins, W. H., Quincy, Ill.
Coon, Peter, Manley, Neb.
Forcht, John, Granville, Ill.
Ford, John J., Streator, Ill.

(101 Illinois Vol. Inf. Continued.)

COMPANY D CONTINUED.

Gage, Richard J., Marseilles, Ill.
Galloway, M. M., 258 E. 64th St., Chicago, Ill.
Gorgenich, John, Chatsworth, Ill.
Greenlees, Wm. A., La Porte, Tex.
Holland, Lemuel F., Bement, Ill.
Houghton, Geo. L., Woodstock, Minn.
Hurin, Alex., Seneca, Ill.
Hutton, James C., Springfield, S. Dak.
Hutton, Lewis K., Omaha, Neb.
Jones, Wm. H., San Jose, Cal.
Jones, Zenas R., Smithdale, Livingston Co., Ill.
Laing, Jos. W., Rensselaer, Ind.
Lane, Marcus J., Ransom, Ill.
Leland, Sherman, Ottawa, Ill.
Makeever, Cyrus H., Marseilles, Ill.
Marcellus, Chas., Stockville, Neb.
Marsh, George, 916 23rd St., Washington, D. C.
McCormick, Wm., Ransom, Ill.
Miller, Melvin P., Salt Lake City, Utah.
Moore, George, Ayr, Neb.
Peters, J., Barton, Kan.
Plowman, J. R., Pontiac, Ill.
Post, John T., Alhambra, Cal.
Powers, John H., Trenton, Neb.
Payne, Samuel B., Waterloo, Neb.
Rathbun, Alonzo E., Soldiers Home, St. Paul, Minn.
Reynolds, Reuben, Hennesey, Okla.
Rinker, John, Marseilles, Ill.
Shapland, John, York, Neb.
Shaub, Bolser, Saunemin, Ill.
Skeel, Oliver M., Sandwich, Ill.
Slagle, Oscar, Kempton, Ill.
Smalley, R. S. Ransom, Ill.
Smith, A. S., Birmingham, Conn.
Smith, F., 212 Prospect St., Council Bluffs, Ia.
Snediker, G. P., Lucas, Ia.
Spink, James, Northfield, Minn.
Stanford, David, Chatsworth, Ill.
Steward, M. H., Philo, Ill.
Taylor, George, Streator, Ill.
Walbridge, O. D., Marseilles, Ill.
Wallace, Lewis F., Piper City, Ill.
Wallace, Robert, Paxton, Neb.
Wilson, Luther A., Furley, Kan.

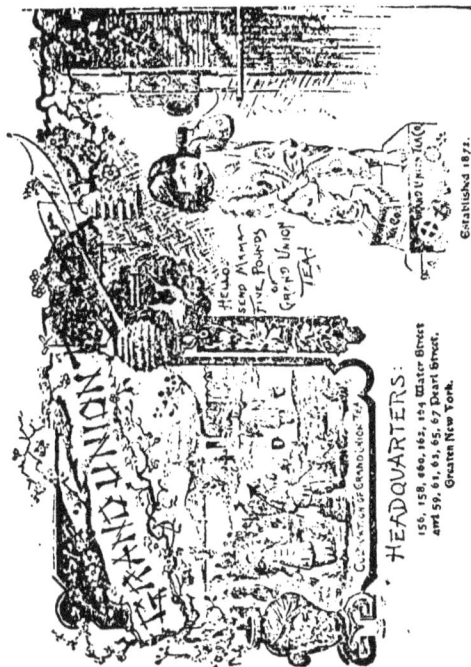

GRAND UNION TEA CO.

The Largest Importers and Retailers of Teas
and Coffees in the United States. We make
a specialty of handling the best goods that
spot cash will buy in the countries where
they are produced. From Plantation to
Consumer—all middle men's profits are
saved. This enables us to sell our goods
at the lowest possible prices. In addition,
we give premiums with all purchases.
When our salesman calls on you, kindly
give him an order, as we know you will be
well pleased. When in Streator call and
see our branch store and be shown the
beautiful presents we are giving to our
many patrons.

GRAND UNION TEA CO.,

Branch Store, 219 East Main Street,

STREATOR,   -   -   -   ILL.

COMPANY E.

Abbott, S. E., Oxford, Neb.
Bailey, John E., Chicago, Ill.
Baumgardner, I. B. Ottawa, Ill.
Breese, S. H. Bancroft, Ia.
Brown, Charles, Ogalalla, Neb.
Calkins, W. W., 117 California Ave., Chicago, Ill.
Conard, Jos.W., Buckley, Ill.
Conard, W. H., Ransom, Ill.
Cunningam Geo. H., unknown.
Cunningham, J. T., Chicago, Ill.
Cummins, Geo. H., San Francisco, Cal.
Dewey, Ransom P., Marseilles, Ill.
Doty, Henry A., Bloomington, Ill.
Downing, Lysander, McMinnville, Ore.
Ellsworth, Willard M., Terre Haute, Ind.
Fisk, Samuel A. Fitzgerald, Ia.
Green, Jas. L., Marseilles, Ill.
Hart, John W., Salem, Kan.
Hills, Jas. M., care Ogden, Sheldon & Co., Chicago, Ill.
Hornbeck, Newton J., Streator, Ill.
Kemp, Albert P., Arkansas City, Kan.
Kimball, Jared K. Moberly, Mo.
Lawrence, James D., Thawville, Ill.
Lyle, James, Aurora, Ill.
Mead, H. L., Tacoma, Wash.
Nattinger, Lyman, San Jose, Cal.
Newell, Augustus, Rockport, Mo.
Newell, J. G., Streator, Ill.
Pembrook, Charles, Ayr, Adams Co., Neb.
Roberts, Alfred, unknown.
Rumple, David, Ottawa, Ill.
Russell, E. C., San Francisco, Cal.
Smith, H. B., Deer Park, Ill.
Smith, Wm. H., Utica, Ill.
Wallace, John, Pontiac, Ill.
Whitman, Q. D., Soldiers Home, Quincy, Ill.
Wilson, C., McCune, Crawford Co., Kan.
Wilson, Jos. B., Utica, Ill.
Wilson, W. M., Spaulding, Ia.
Wisher, David A., Centralia, Ill.
Wyman, Evan, Omaha, Neb.
Wilsey, Almon C., Chicago, Ill.
Zeek, Darwin, Amboy, Ill.

JOHN ESSINGTON,

Loans and

Real Estate.

City and Farm Property a Specialty,

STREATOR.   ILLINOIS.

L. L. GRAVES,

Machine Shops, Iron and Brass Foundries.

Hoisting Engines,   *Ventilating Fans,*
Sheave Wheels,
Steam Pumps,   *Jet Pumps,*   *Pit Cars,*
Bronze and Brass Castings,
Car Wheels.   *Columns-Lintels,*
Door Plates,   *Boiler Fronts, Etc.*

OFFICE AND WORKS,

Cor. Hickory and Wason Sts., STREATOR, ILL.

(101 Illinois Vol. Inf. Continued.)

COMPANY F.

Ackerman, Henry, Grant, Ia.
Ayers, Joshua, Mt. Auburn, Ia.
Bardwell, A. G., Galesburg, Neosho Co., Kan.
Birtwell, Robert, Streator, Ill.
Brown, William, Kernan, Ill.
Burns, William, Long Point, Ill.
Caldwell, William, Streator, Ill.
Campbell, William, Streator, Ill.
Clark, Orrin, Homer, Mich.
Cooper, John, Sunrise, Ill.
Cooper, William, Streator, Ill.
Crider, Martin H., Otter, Ill.
Clode, T. J., Harbine, Neb.
Daugherty, F. M., Streator, Ill.
Ewing, John K., Shannon City, Ia.
Flanagan, William, Streator, Ill.
Gatchell, James M., Marseilles, Ill.
Green, Samuel, Gilman, Ill.
Goodman, Wm., Palmyro, Mo.
Hart, Girard, unknown.
Head, William, Bedford, Ia.
Holland, John, Esmond, DeKalb Co., Ill.
Hopple, Jerry, Toluca, Ill.
Hurst, William, Cleveland, Minn.
Kiner, Samuel A. Grand Ridge, Ill.
Lindsley, J. C., Stevenson, Tex.
Long, William, Rensselaer, Ind.
Mackey, Charles, Streator, Ill.
Mackey, Geo. W., Streator, Ill.
McCashland, Ed., Sutton, Neb.
Mooney, James, Shannon City, Ia.
Musberger, George, Vincent, Ill.
Pool, Robert, Sunrise, Ill.
Pressor, John, Streator, Ill.
Rodehofer, David, Chicago, Ill.
Rude, Squire, Pekin, Ill.
Rush, Nicholas, Streator, Ill.
Ryerson, Thomas, Cornell, Ill.
Shay, John H., Streator, Ill.
Strawn, William, Odell, Ill.
Thompson, Thomas, Badger, Ia.
Wilson, Hugh H., 135 Castor St., Pittsburg, Pa.

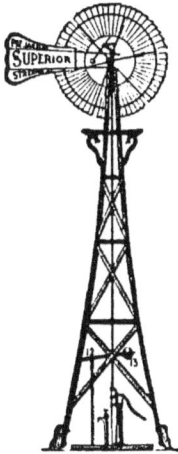

(104 Illinois Vol. Inf. Continued.)

COMPANY G.

Bagwill, Marshall, Millington, Ill.
Blackburn, John, Dorchester, Neb.
Bullard, Ed. S., Millbrook, Ill.
Brown, A. L. Marseilles, Ill.
Brown, Amos E., Tocoma, Wash.
Campbell, Hamilton, Anita, Ia.
Campbell, John H., Streator, Ill.
Cairns, James C., Des Moines, Ia.
Cartwright, C. C., Sandwich, Ill.
Close, William, Sandwich, Ill.
Cook, C. B, Los Angeles, Cal.
Campbell, Wm., Streator, Ill.
Deegan, James, C., Ransom, Ill.
Diehl, Jacob F., Nelson, Neb.
Dinger, Peter, Gilman, Ill.
Eastwood, A. J., Streator, Ill.
Fullerton, B. S., Peabody, Kan.
Fullerton, T. C., unknown.
Gillam, John C., Radcliffe, Ia.
Gillam, O. B., Hubbard, Ia.
Hawk, Phil. A. Mankato, Kan.
Haney, S. B., Elkhorn, Neb.
Jones, W. M., Grand Ridge, Ill.
Lewis, Geo. F., Montana.
Mason, Daniel, Ottawa, Ill.
McCleary, Charles, Dwight, Ill.
McKinnell, William, Millersburg, Ill.
McQuown, M. Glasford, Ill.
Misner, G. D., Kinsley, Kan.
Misner, Jeptha, Newark, Ill.
Misner, John N., Millington, Ill.
Nelson, C. C., Randall, Ia.
Overmire, Jacob, J., Anita, Ia.
Porter, Samuel B., unknown.
Pound, Frank S., Iona, Jewell Co., Kan.
Richardson, John, Streator, Ill.
Richardson, Ole, Fairmount, Neb.
Rood, H. A., Seneca, Ill.
Rood, Jas. P., Lerville, Idaho.
Rowe, Alfred, Currant Creek, Freemont Co., Col.
Rowe, James L., Sheridan, Ill.
Ruble, John, Klla, S. Dak.
Sampson, Simeon, Kernan, Ill.
Scott, Ephriam, Lake Arthur, La.
Sibert, Andrew S, Waterloo, Neb.
Tice, Alonzo A., Marseilles, Ill.
Trice, Lewis E., Goodland, Ind.
Trice, Wm. E., Goodland, Ind.
Weidknecht, William, Utica, Ill.
White, Selim, Wilmington, Ill.

OTTAWA.

(104 Illinois Vol. Inf. Continued.)

COMPANY H.

Adams, Thomas, Washington, Kan.
Bane, James, Dana, Ill.
Bosley, Hawey M., Oklahoma City, Okla.
Brown, Samuel, Wenona, Ill.
Bosley, Morris M., Magnolia, Ill.
Ball, Samuel, Decatur, Ill.
Cunningham, S. H., Chillicothe, Ill.
Dillman, W. P., Nevada, Ill.
Dixon, Geo., Melvin, Ill.
Donney, Reuben, Mound City, Mo.
Donney, Neal, Minneapolis, Minn.
Doninick, Geo. W. Wichita, Kan.
Ellis, H. R., Cornell, Ill.
Everitt, H. S., Great Bend, Kan.
Earl, W. D., York, Neb.
Everitt, John, Great Bend, Kan.
Fowler, A. H., Slayton, Minn.
Griffin, Geo. W., Wenona, Ill.
Hunt, W. J, Melvin, Ford Co., Ill.
Hammitt, Geo. W., Smithville, Ill.
Laughman, William, Harlan, Ia.
Luddington, Lewis, Lafayette, Ind.
Merritt, J. E. Hutchinson, Kan.
Miller, A. P., Eldorado, Kan.
Miller, Harrison, Silver City, Ia.
Mills, Lewis C., Reading, Ill.
Moore, E. S., Gravity, Ia.
Nelson, Henry, Rutland, Ill.
Odes, Jos. T., Bolivar, Mo.
Philson, J. W., Dodge, Neb.
Porter, Abe, Sandstone, Mo.
Ream, W. C., Joliet, Ill.
Rector, Newton, Hennesey, Okla.
Stire, Frank H., Apolis Junction, Ind.
Vaughn, Isaac, Wenona, Ill.
Williamson, J. B., Sac City, Ia.
Wilson, Thomas, Corning, Ia.
Work, James, S., Wenona, Ill.
Wolf, X., 589 Miama, St., Indianapolis, Ind.
Wells, L. C., Reading, Ill.

COL. J. B. PARSONS,

Pres. of The Union Envelope Co., Pontiac, Ilinois.

Late Sergt. Co. A, 1st Maine Heavy Artillery.

Late Colonel 10th Infantry, I. N. G.

Past Commander Post 626, Dept. of Illinois,

Aide-de-camp to Department Commander.

✳

Patriotic   Printing.

✳

300,000 ENVELOPES PRINTED IN
BEAUTIFUL COLORS AND PATRIOTIC DESIGNS
CARRIED IN STOCK.

Send 20 Cents for 25 Varieties.

THE UNION ENVELOPE CO.,
PONTIAC, ILLINOIS,

COMPANY I.

Allen, David, Miltonvale, Kan.
Bailey, Andrew J., Norda, Ia.
Bailey, John, Pontiac, Ill.
Baker, Vil., Mendota, Ill.
Bane, Jacob, Springfield, Ill.
Callaghan, Anthony, Richland, Minn.
Collins, Andrew, Peoria, Ill.
Cooper, John, Long Point, Ill.
Cooper, Nelson H., Rutland, Ill.
Everetts, Richard, Rutland, Ill.
Foster, Samuel, Holder, Ill.
Frink, W. E., Wartsburg, Wash.
Harkness, Porter, Englewood, Ill.
Lakin, William, Dorchester, Neb.
Lamp, Charles, Bloomington, Ill.
Lewis, Geo. E., Ottawa, Ill.
Mallory, Erastus F., Hamilton, Ia.
McFadden, F. D., Laramie City, Wyo.
Merritt, Malley, Streator, Ill.
Moffitt, Andrew, Dorchester, Neb.
Mullen, N. H., Los Angeles, Cal.
Powell, J. C., Dana, Ill.
Proctor, Willard, Gibson City, Ill.
Purviance, Mark, Cromwell, Ia.
Purviance, W., Clinton, Ia.
Quinlan, John, Parsons, Kan.
Rice, Charles, Bloomington, Ill.
Robinson, O. L., Wenona, Ill.
Showman, H. P., Streator, Ill.
Smack, Abraham, Wood, Ia.
Smith, A. T., Pinconning, Mich.
Thompson, Jerry, LeMars, Ia.
Trask, D. F., Cimarron, Kan.
Travers, J. J., Varna, Ill.
Wadleigh, John, Rutland, Ill.
Winans, R. B., Fonda, Ia.
Wright, Jas. M., Hams Fork, Uinta Co., Wyo.

COMPANY K.

Alexander, Geo. K., Dubuque, Ia.
Barton, William, Parsons, Kan.
Bell, James, Kempton, Ill.
Bell, Robert, Chatsworth, Ill.
Burkhart, Joseph, LaSalle, Ill.
Bushnell, Milton B. Chicago, Ill.
Butterweck, Charles, Florid, Putnam Co., Ill.
Carney, Joseph, Steward, Lee Co., Ill.
Chapin, Henry A., 4312 Cottage Grove, Ave., Chicago,
    Ill.
Conley, Thos. S., Maple Rock, Ia.
Duffy, Joseph, La Salle, Ill.
Engel, Louis, unknown.
Entzminger, John, 1194 Wilton Ave., Chicago, Ill.
Favor, Otis S., 8 Wabash Ave., Chicago, Ill.
Finhold, Frederick, Kenwood, Ia.
Hahn, George, Hollowayville, Ill.
Hoss, Edward, Cabery, Ill.
Kohr, John H., Peru, Ill.
Lindemeier, John, Beloit, Kan.
Maurer, Frank, Peru, Ill.
McConnell, John M., Meridan, Ia.
McLain, Otho L., 910 Ann St., Kansas City, Kan.
Merkel, Henry, Peru, Ill.
Moffitt, Eli R., Adrian, Mich.
O'Laublin, Michael, Emington, Ill.
Palmer, J. W., Ashland, Neb.
Pitzer, George, Wedron, Ill.
Rhan, Nathan, La Salle, Ill.
Ryan, Cornelius, Ames, Neb.
Sapp, Frank M., Ottawa, Ill.
Slyder, Luther F., Webster City, Ia.
Stroble, J. G., Humbolt, Kan.
Sutcliffe, Benjamin, Hennepin, Ill.
Trompeter, Frank, Peoria, Ill.
Trompeter, J. P., Baker, Kan.
Winslow, William, Freeport, Ill.

Mexican War Soldiers Now Living at Streator.

Andrew J. Baker, private Co. E, 4th Ohio Vol. Inf.,
pension attorney.
Levi Clay, —— retired farmer.

Union Soldiers Now Living at Streator

Not Members of the Local Grand Army Post.

W. A. Bronson, private B, 127 N. Y. Inf., retired.
John M. Hunter, private C, 182 Ohio Inf., mason.
Lewis T. Morgan, private E, 8 Ill. Inf, carpenter.
Conrad Geiger, private B, 6 N. Y. Inf., agent.
J. E. Buchanan, private I, 53 Ill. Inf., plasterer.
Jno. S. Hindman, private E, 140 Pa. Inf., carpenter.
Wm. Cadwell, private F, 104 Ill. Inf., stock buyer.
James Jones, private A, 4 W. Va. Inf., miner.
Jas. Carrington, private F, 33 Ill. Inf., laborer.
W. A. Johnston, private F, 27 Pa. Inf., merchant.
D. S. Carmony, private E, 26 Ill. Inf., mail carrier.
Patrick Boyle, private K, 90 Ill. Inf., constable.
Geo. A. Crowl, private G, 20 Ohio Inf., farmer.
John W. Beath, private D, 48 Ohio Inf., tinner.
Timothy Hallisey, private G, 32 Mass. Inf., laborer.
Wm. Burrell, private G, 33 Ill Inf., coal operator.
Henry Shannon, private C, 8 Ill. Inf., shoemaker.
Martin Mohler, private G, 2 Ohio Inf., harness maker.
Stephen B. Patterson, private D, 52 Ill. Inf., laborer.
Geo. H. Stout, plumber.
Robert Law, carpenter.
W. S. Cherry, U. S. Navy, Coal Co. supt.
Albert Risley.

LA SALLE.

Officers, Past Post Commanders and Members of

Carter Post No. 242 G. A. R.

LA SALLE, ILLINOIS.

Organized June 11th, 1883.

OFFICERS.

J. A. Ramsey............................Commander
W. E. Chapin.................Sen. Vice Commander
Miles Boland................Junior Vice Commander
W. F. Corbus..............................Surgeon
W. H. Hunter.............................Chaplain
T. M. Page ....Adjutant
Joseph Burkart......................Quartermaster
John Sullivan ....Officer of the Day
John Fuchs............ ....Officer of the Guard
Mathew Weast.................... ....Sergt. Major
Joseph Littan.................Quartermaster Sergt

PAST POST COMMANDERS.

A. J. Reddick,   Michael Loos,
Lawrence Morrissey,   S. C. Lambert,
A. J. Reed,   W. E. Chapin,
      John A. Ramsey.

W. H. Hunter & Co,

(Successors to JOHN STUART,)

LUMBER, LATH
and SHINGLES.

Lime, Hair,
Cement, Hard Coal.

Estimates Furnished.

OFFICE, 136 Hennepin Street,

LA SALLE, - ILL.

THE HYGIENIC SUPPLY EMPORIUM,

Dr. R. M. Sterrett, Manager.

Represents reliable Manufacturers ONLY. All goods GUARAN-
TEED as represented, or money refunded.

WE WANT AGENTS!

Good, honest, industrious agents. Men and women
in every city, town and village and in the country
to show, introduce and sell our goods. As we
control EXCLUSIVE territory, we can give you
the best opportunity you ever had to make money,
QUICKLY, HONORABLY AND WITHOUT
Capital. We don't offer you a chance to make a
fortune without work—Better avoid any one who
does. But if you are sensible and in earnest, we
can help you to make from $20.00 to $40.00 per
week. You CAN'T LOSE, because we are backed
by over $100,000.00 capital and all the goods we
handle are GUARANTEED OR MONEY RE-
funded. We will not do business with any other
class of manufacturers.
DON'T PUT IT OFF. WRITE US TO-DAY. START
A BUSINESS OF YOUR OWN— YOU MAKE ALL THE
PROFIT ON YOUR LABOR. Address,

THE HYGIENIC SUPPLY EMPORIUM,

Lock Box 653,   -   LA SALLE, ILL.

Burkart, Joseph, private Co. K, 104 Ill., asst. supervisor

Boland, Miles, private Co. C, 44th Ill., farmer.

Corbus, W. F., Hospital Steward, 75th Ill., druggist.

Chapin, W. E., private Co. L., 58 N. Y. Light Art., farmer.

Clinch, Thomas, private Troop A, 9th Ill. Cav., engineer.

Fuchs, John, Lieut. Co. A, 44th Ill., laborer.

Garfield, F. M., private Co. G, 23rd Ill., express agt.

Hunter, W. H., Corp. Co. I, 94th Ill., lumber.

Littau, Joseph, private Co. F, 2nd Mo. Art., laborer.

Lambert, S. C., Co. F, 10th Ill. Inf., carpenter.

Landers, William, private Co. B, 165 Pa., carpenter.

Morrissey, Lawrence, private Co. H. 90th Ill., deputy sheriff.

Page, Thomas M., 2nd Lieut Co. E, 9th Ky. Cav., R. R. employ.

Ramsey, A. J., private Co. C, 1st Ill. Light Art., secretary.

Reed, A. J., private Co. M, 3rd Pa. Cav., miner.

Sullivan, John, private Co. E, 16th N. Y. Inf., miner.

Sanders, Joseph, Sergt. Co. K, 53rd Ill., carpenter.

Willer, N. J., Sergt. Co. I, 53rd Ill., carpenter.

Weast, Mathew, private Co. C, 31st Wis., laborer.

MAJOR B. F. BUTLER.

Union Soldiers Buried in St. Vincent Cemetery, La Salle, Illinois.

John Mellon, Co. G, 55th Ill., died July 28, 1887.
Michael McDermott, Co. K, 104 Ill.
Philip Gorman, Co. A, 58th Ill.
Dennis Humphry, Co. H, 11th Ill. Inf.
John Allen, Co. H, 58th Ill.
Thomas Clear.
John Noonan, Sergt. Co. K, 90th Ill.
Martin Hanley.
William Welch.
Nicholas Geib, Co. I, 2nd Wis. Inf.
Patrick Gorman, Co. A, 58th Ill.
Patrick A. Holligan, Co. C, 9th Ill. Cav.
William Lyons.
Michael Noon, Co. H, 58th Ill.
Thomas C. Murray.
D. L. Callahan, Co. H, 7th Kan.
Richard Waters, Co. K, 11th Ill. Inf.
James McCabe.
Timothy Cremin.
William Pittz.
James Carey.
I. Collins, Co. H, 58th Ill.
John Collins, Co. H, 58th Ill.
John Cummings.
Timothy Sullivan.

Union Soldiers Buried in Oak Wood Cemetery, La Salle, Illinois.

A. J. Reddick, Co. F, 107 Pa., died March 31, 1889.
J. C. Brown, war of 1812, died June 12, 1883.
Benj. Doll, Co. G, 6th Minn. Inf.
Joseph Diggle, Co. B, 8th Pa. Cav.

Union Soldiers Buried in Oak Hill Cemetery, Utica, Illinois.

Leander Smith, C, 1st Ill. Art.
Wm. H. Baldwin, K, 11 Ill. Inf.
Frank Nichols, D, 107 Ill Inf., died January 20, 1886.
Leander Tate, H, 11 Ill. Inf., died January 5, 1873.
James Wright, Henshaws Ill. Battery.
Thos. L. Height, died February 25, 1891.
Benjamin D. Carlisle, F, 1 R. I. Inf., died June 4, 1893.
D. O. Collins, F, 64 Ill. Inf., died April 29, 1887.
George W. White, I, 53 Ill. Inf., died February 3, 1889.
William McCauslin, M, 6, U. S. Cav., died Nov. 7, 1895.
Joseph Stoebel, Cogswells, Ill. Battery, died May 20, 1897.
John Isham.
Lewis M. Smith, Battery C, 1st Ill. Art.

Union Soldiers Buried in Troy Grove Cemetery.

Wm. Baker, 64 Ill. Inf.
E. C. McLaughlin 12 Ill. Inf.
Peter Scholtz, Co. K, 104 Ill., died April 30, 1888.
John Teed, 55 Ill. Inf.
Frank Foster 64 Ill. Inf.
Joseph Shepard, 53 Ill. Inf.
J. E. Wilkins, C, 104 Ill. Inf.
Joseph Edwards, 55 Ill. Inf.
Henry McLaren, Pa. Inf.
John Simpson, war of 1812.

Prairie Center Cemetery.

George Day, A, 64 Ill. Inf, died August 11, 1864.
Ira Longer, Capt. A, 64 Ill. Inf., died Oct. 18, 1864.
Wm. H. Hinkley, A, 64 Ill. Inf., died June 27, 1864.
Francis A. Kellogg, A, 64 Ill. Inf., died Jan. 9, 1877.
Melvin R. Butterfield, A, 64 Ill. Inf., died June 6, 1862.
Thos. W. Lukins, A, 64 Ill. Inf., died Dec. 9, 1862.
Chas. Barstons, A, 64 Ill. Inf., died June 6, 1862.
S. W. Fogg, 12 U. S. Inf , died November 11, 1866.
Robert Campbell, B, 9 Mich. Cav., died April 9, 1892.
William H. Herbert, C, 76, Ill. Inf., died Mch. 10, 1887.

PERU.

Officers, Past Post Commanders and Members of

E. N. Kirk Post No. 656 G. A. R.

PERU, ILLINOIS.

Organized March 14th, 1888.

OFFICERS.

Wilson J. Morrow ....Commander
Jacob Phillips..................Sen. Vice Commander
Christian Haas..............Junior Vice Commander
William Walther.....................Adjutant
Charles Climo.....................Quartermaster
M. E. Loos................................Surgeon
Daniel Shaffer............................Chaplain
Eric Nelson...................Officer of the Day
Dennis Manning.................Officer of the Guard
——————..............................Sergt. Major
Geo. Schreiber...............Quartermaster Sergeant

PAST POST COMMANDERS.

M. E. Loos,   G. Gmelick,
A. Means,   Jacob Phillips,
        John H. Kohr.

MEMBERS.

Babcock, William, private Co. B, 104 Ill., farmer.
Boeckling, Adam, private Co. A, 44th Ill., painter.
Birkembevel, F., private Co. A, 44th Ill., mason.
Climo, Charles, Sergt. Co. B, 1st Mo. Inf., merchant.
Denney, F. J., private Co. B, 127th Ill., weigh master.
Eisfold, H., private Co. A, 44th Ill., wagon maker.
Griffith, Robert, private Co. H, 110 Ill., weigh master.
Haas, Christian, private Co. A, 44th Ill., merchant.
Holbrook, Jerry, private Co. E, 93rd Ill., teamster.
Heck, William, private Co., A, 44th Ill., farmer.
Kohr, John H, private Co. K, 104 Ill., laborer.
Kizer, Charles, Co. E, 4th Ill. Cav., farmer.

(E. N. Kirk Post No. 656 G. A. R., Continued.)

Kinckle, Wm., private Co. G, 11th Ill. Inf., farmer.
Loos, M. E., Lieut. Co. H, 34th Ill., farmer.
Loner, Otto, private Co. A, 44th Ill., livery.
Leyes, Joseph, private Co. E, 44th Ill., farmer.
Lavitt, John, private Co. I, 12th N. Il. Inf., farmer.
Morrow, Wilson J., private Co. A, 8th Ill. Cav., farmer.
Manning, Dennis, private Co. K, 11th Ill. Inf., black-
    smith.
Mauer, Frank, private Co. K, 104 Ill., engineer.
Merkle, Henry, private Co H, 104 Ill., restaurant.
Newton, W. W., private Co. K, 34th Ill., laborer.
Nelson, Eric, Corp. Co. D, 36th Ill., tailor.
Noal, John, private Co. E, 76th Ill., laborer.
Phillips, Jacob, private Battery A, 3rd Ill. Art., me-
    chinist.
Schreiber, Geo., private Co. K, 11th Wis., laborer.
Shaffer, David, private Co. K, 104 Ill., merchant.
Walther, William, private Co. A, 44th Ill., agent.

Union Soldiers now Living in Peru

Not Members of the Local Grand Army Post.

H. S. Corwin, private Battery D, 1st Ill. Light Art.,
    postmaster.
Ivery S. Cole, private Co. C, 198 Ohio, physician.
Samuel Hicks, private Co. B, 127 Ill., painter.
John Wart, U. S. Navy, miner.
Michael Christopher, private Co. E, 2nd Ky. Cav.,
    laborer.
Henry Ziesing, Surgeon 53rd Ill., physician.
John A. Helfrish, private Co. G, 189 Ohio, teamster.
William Ulrick, private Co. B, 7th Ky., miner.
John Rhm, Corp. Co. C, 1st Mo. Art., cooper.
Herman Strauver, private Co. A, 44th Ill., painter.

Union Soldiers Buried in City Cemetery,
Peru.

Chris Funk, Co. H, 210 Pa., died Nov. 5, 1898.
Chris Langenfler, Co. A, 44th Ill., died Dec. 6, 1898.
John Engee, Co. E, 44th Ill., died March 17, 1890.
Albright Koehler, Co. A, 53rd Ill., died Dec. 1, 1891.
A. Means, Capt. Co. E, 11th Ky. Inf., died May 22, 1898.
G. Ginelick, Corp. Co. A, 11th Ill., died April 21, 1898.
Peter Scholtz, Co. K, 104 Ill., died in 1887.
Levi C. Scott, Co. K, 25th Ill., died June 9, 1897.
J. W. Simmons, Sergt. Co. F, 7th Ohio Inf., died June
    1, 1898.
Henry Durnbush, Co. A, 44th Ill., died Nov. 25, 1897
John Miller, U. S. Navy, died Jan. 14, 1896.
Martin Malock, Co. K, 104 Ill., died April 28, 1893.
George Morrison, Co. D, 2nd Iowa Cav.
Peter J. Saszenburg, Co. E, 44th Ill., buried in Catholic
    Cemetery.

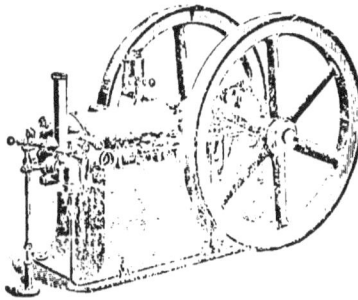

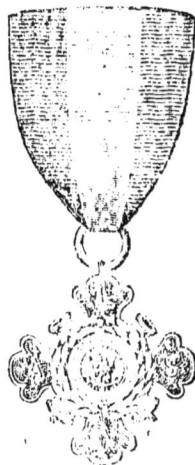

Officers and Members of

Ladies Aid Society No. 11,

PERU, ILLINOIS.

Organized April 25th, 1899.

OFFICERS.

Emma Weberling............... ....President
Emma Phillips...................... Vice President
Susie Climo................................Treasurer
Marguerite Walther... ....Secretary
Ella Conradi............................Chaplain
Nettie Morrow........................... .. .Guide
Etta Shaffer........................Assistant Guide
Clara Walther........................Inside Guard
Maggie Morrow................... ...Outside Guard

TRUSTEES.

Hulda Birkenbeul,   Mary Walther,
          Elena Gallagher.

PAST PRESIDENT.

Dora Eisfelt.

MEMBERS.

Dora Eisfelt,	Louisa Wasson,
Mary Walther,	Emma Zacker,
Clara Walther,	Elena Gallagher,
Mary Louer,	Lizzie Ugel,
Mrs. Adolph Hoss,	Ella Conradi,
Susen Climo,	Mrs. Wm. A. Loos,
Maggie Morrow,	Emma Weberling.
Nettie Morrow,	Marguerite Walther,
Mrs. A. Means,	Etta Shaffer,
Julia Walthers,	Mary Puttcamp,
Hulda Birkenbeul,	Mrs. T. F. Noon.
Mrs. G. Gmelick,	Jessie Means.

.

Officers and Members of

Captain Archibald Means Camp
No. 116 Sons of Veterans,

PERU, ILLINOIS.

Organized October 8th, 1898.

OFFICERS.

Eugene Morrow..............................Captain
Alfred Walthers......................1st Lieutenant
A. H. Puttcamp......................2d Lieutenant
W. F. Eisfeld...........................1st Sergeant
Edward Zechler..................Sergt. of the Guard
W. H. Noon........................Q. M. Sergeant
Alvin Ramsey................................Chaplin
John Karp....................Corp. of the Guard
Otto Eisfeld............................Color Sergeant
Joseph Knoll...........................Camp Guard
Edward Streaver.........................Picket Guard

MEMBERS.

Eisfeld, Wm. F.,
Eisfeld, Otto,
Hoss, Adolph,
Korp, John,
Knoll, Joseph,
Kohr, John A,
Landis, Henry J.,
Loos, W. A. J.,
Morrow, Eugene,
Maurer, George,
Maurer, John,
Maurer, W.,
Morrow, Arthur,
Noon, W. H.,
Noon, Thos. F.,
Puttcamp, Albert H.,
Philips, Charles,
Ramsey, Alvin,
Streaver, Edward,
Walthers, Alfred,
Zechler, Edward,
Zoehler, Gilbert.

MARSEILLES.

Joseph Woodruff Post No. 281,

MARSEILLES, ILLINOIS.

Organized June 18th, 1883.

OFFICERS.

D. A. Kerns............................Commander
William Sindel................Sen. Vice Commander
J. W. Greene...............Junior Vice Commander
M. J. Bosworth ....Adjutant
Geo. B. Bignall..... ....Surgeon
A. F. Brown................................Chaplain
B. A. Roath..........................Quartermaster
J. W. Preston.....................Officer of the Day
C. H. McKeever... ....Officer of the Guard
O. L. Fuller............................Sergt. Major
J. Hill.............. ....Q. M. Sergeant

PAST POST COMMANDERS.

Geo. L. Danison,	A. L. Stone,
John D. McKahin,	O. L. Fuller,
Ransom P Dewey,	M. J. Bosworth,
David H. Slagle,	Geo. B. Bignall,
J. W. Preston,	D. A. Nicholson,
O. B. Grant.	

MEMBERS.

Adams, J. Q., Lieut. and Q. M. 53rd Ill., manufacturer.
Allen, J. H., Lieut. Co. L, 11th Ill. Cav., druggist.
Bignall, Geo. B., Corp. Co. H, 11th Ill. Inf., engineer.
Babcock, Thos. B., private Co. E, 26th Ill. Inf., farmer.
Butterfield, P. A., Corp., Co. A, Fords Cav., farmer.
Brown, A. F., Sergt. Co. E. 26th Ill., Gardener.
Barber, J. L., private Co. L, 15th Ill. Cav., farmer.
Bevington, Joel, private Co. C, 50th Ohio, farmer.
Bosworth, G. A., Corp. Co. A, Fords Cav., farmer.
Bosworth, M. J., private Co. L, 15th Ill. Cav., farmer.
Babcock, Chas., private Co. E, 26th Ill., laborer.
Cooper, J. S., private Co. I, 138 Ill., teamster.
Cuddaback, M. P., private Co. A, 64th Ill., farmer.
Davidson, G. L., 1st Lieut. Co. B, 99th Ohio, police
    magistrate.
Dewey, R. P., Capt. Co E, 104 Ill., carpenter.
Danley, S. K., private Co. F, 1st Regt. U. S. Eng., Car-
    penter.
Fuller, O. L., private Co. C, 88th Ill., machinist.
Grout, O. B., private Co. C, 53rd Ill., police magistrate.
Gum, A. S., private Co. C, 72nd Ill., florist.
Greene, J. W., private Co. C, 4th Ill. Cav., farmer.
Gage, R. J., private Co. D, 104 Ill., farmer.
Hubbard, Albert, private Co. K, 39th Ill., lock tender..
Hattes, Eber, private Co. C, 53rd Ill., laborer.
Hill, J. F., private Co. B, 9th Mich. Inf., laborer.
Knox, Isaac, private Co. G, 3rd Minn. Inf., flag man.
Kerns, D. A., private Co. D, 52nd Ohio, mechanic.
Kline, Tobias, private Co. D, 64th U. S. Inf., farmer.
Makeever, S. L., Corp. Co E, 153 Ill., farmer.
Makeever, C. H., Corp. Co. D, 104 Ill., farmer.
Nicholson, D. A., Capt. Co. E, 153rd Ill., city attorney.
Nickerbocker, Nelson, private Co. G, 53rd Ill., blind.
Oleson, Jacob, private Co. K, 39th, Ill. Inf., mason.
Preston, J. W., Lieut. U. S. C, Inf., merchant.
Pitts, F. D., private Chicago Mercantile Battery, man-
    ufacturer.
Penfield, C. W., private Co. G, 116 N. Y., merchant.
Roath, B. A., Sergt. Co. F, 9th Mich. Inf., J. P.
Richmond, W. H., private Co. E, 91st Ill., lock tender.
Slagle, D. H., Sergt. Co. K, 39th Ill., mail Agent.
Smith, M. P., private Co. F, 138 Ill., mechanic.
Smith, L. W., private Co G, 129 Ill., carpenter.
Snidel, W. H, Sergt. Co. F, 67th Ohio, farmer.
Thurber, O. P., Corp. Co. I, 138 Ill., carpenter.
Thomas, Cyrus, Lieut. Co. B, 11th Vt. Inf., clergyman.
Worthingham, W. B., private Co. B. 20th Ill. Inf.,
    painter.
Wilson, Enoch, private Co. F, 11th Ill. Cav., mechanist.

Officers, Past Presidents and Members of

Joseph Woodruff W. R. C. No. 94,

MARSEILLES, ILLINOIS.

Organized January 12th, 1888.

OFFICERS.

Julina Hayes............................President
Mary Tice.....................Sen. Vice President
Anna Messenie..............Junior Vice President
Susie Adams...............................Secretary
Celia Dewey. .. ..Treasurer
Amanda Roath............................Chaplain
Mary Kelley...............................Conductor
Jennie Swingler..............................Guard
Roxy Bignall... ....Assist. Conductor
Mary Harder ....Assist. Guard

PAST PRESIDENTS.

Mary Stone,   Amanda Roath,
Elvira Porter,   Mary Tice,
Celia Dewey,   Roxy Bignall.

MEMBERS.

Mary Stone,   Sarah Butterfield,
Amanda Roath,   Lizzie Bevington,
Elvira Porter,   Julina Hayes,
Amanda Barber,   Hannah McCutcheon,
Emeline Wilson,   Emma Whitman,
Mary Harder,   Greta Daley,
Caroline Daley,   Ruth Hayes,
Mattie Hill,   Mary Cuddaback,
Emily Grant,   Nancy Richmond,
Celia Dewey,   Mary Hill,
Minnie Bosworth,   Jennie Swingler,
Mary Tice,   Ella Wilson,
Abbie Gum,   Anna Messenie,
Roxy Bignall,   Laura Gage,
Delia Hogue,   Caroline Klein,
Mary Kelley,   Ellen Makeever,
Martha Hanlon,   Alida Sindel,
Susie Adams,   Harriet Makeever,
　　　　Alice Keesler.

E. A. GRANT & CO.,

GROCERIES and NOTIONS,

No. 5, Brick Block.

Telephone No. 89.

Marseilles, · · Ill,

C. M. BENSON,

The Practical Tailor of Marseilles, can always be depended on to give full value and satisfaction.

ARTHUR GUM.

HOUSE and CARRIAGE PAINTING.

Good work at reasonable prices. Shop on Main Street.

MARSEILLES, · · ILL.

A. E. HANES,

Dealer in

OILS and NON-EXPLOSIVE GASOLINE.

930 Union Street, MARSEILLES, ILL.

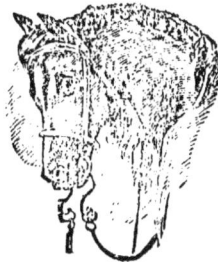

Union Soldiers now Living at Marseilles

Not Members of the Local G. A. R. Post.

Walbridge, O. D., private Co. D, 104 Ill., agent.
Bangham, G. K., Lieut. Co. A, 9th Mich. Inf., mechanic.
Hayes, E. T., private, Co. C, 7th Ohio Inf., carpenter.
Trumble, C. W., Musician 114th N. Y., machinist.
Wilson, Martin, Lieut. Co. F, 36th Ill., merchant.
Butterfield, F. L., private Co. K, 39th Ill., city treas.
Tice, A. A., private Co. G, 104 Ill., mechanic.
Luce, C. E., private Co. K, 104 Ill., laborer.
Gatchell, J. M., private Co. F, 104 Ill., farmer.
Rinker, C. A., private Co. C, 1st Ill. Art., retired farmer
Flanery, Thos., private Co. F, 72d Ill., laborer.
Smith, O. A., Musician 9th Mich. Inf., janitor.
Sparks, S. J., private Co. F, 53d Ill., well driller.
McCutcheon, James, Co. A, 111 N. Y. Inf., moulder
Smouse, Daniel, Lieut. Co. K, 39th Ill., retired farmer.
Holtom, Rachab, Sergt. Co. K, 3rd Del. Inf., laborer.
Long, Samuel, Sergt. Co. A, 3rd Wis. Cav., laborer.
Ivers, C. W., Corp. Co. E, 25th Ill. laborer.
Smith, L. A., private Co. F, 75th N. Y., painter.
Hill, J. F., private Co. F, 9th Mich. Inf., laborer.
Crowell, A. D., private Co. B, 88th Ill., carpenter.
Van Camp, Lyman, Co. 1st Colo. Cav., paper maker
Cothrin, David, C gswells Battery, laborer.
Lace, Daniel, private Cogswells Battery, farmer.
Rinker, John, private Co. D, 104 Ill., farmer.

Union Soldiers buried in old Christian Church Cemetery near Marseilles.

Judson Van Stillwagner, Co. L, 15th Ohio Cav.
Geo. Pollock, Co. K, 39th Ill.
Alonson Pope, Co. C, 88th Ill.

METHODIST EPISCOPAL CHURCH CEMETERY.

Aaron Crandle, Co. C, 88th Ill.
John Holley, Co. C, 88th Ill.
Henry V. Thompson, Co. K, 53th Ill.

HARRINGTONS CEMETERY.

John B. Sparks, Co. K, 39th Ill.

BLUFF CEMETERY.

Nick Ragan.
Henry Grese, Co. G, 13th Ill. Cav.
Zina Ward, Lieut. Co. E, 153 Ill. Inf.
Solan Lowery, Co. G, 92nd N. Y. Inf.
Carlos Morgon, Co. K, 39th Ill. Inf.
Orlando Olmstead, Co. K, 39th Ill. Inf.
Christian Long, private Co. C, 100 Ill. Inf.
Porter Hubbard private Co. I, 8th Ill. Cav.
Otho H. Hobart, drummer Co. D, 104 Ill Inf.
J. S. Blanchard, private 46th Ill. Inf.
Chas. Daley, private C, 88th Ill. Inf.
Edward Strait, private Co. F, 36th Ill. Inf.
O. B. Bignall, Corp. Co. K, 39th Ill. Inf.
Joseph Woodruff, Capt. Co. K, 39th Ill. Inf.
Bur Fleming, private Co. E, 153 Ill. Inf.
John H. Richmond, private Co. E, 91st Ill Inf.
Hiram Whitman, private Co. E, 23rd Ill. Inf.
James S. Sanborn, private Co. K, 39th Ill. Inf.
Felix Zigler, private Co. E, 26th Ill. Inf.
Genoa Brundage.
Chas. Percil.
David Hecox, private Co. A, 5th Bat. N. Y. Art.
Louis Werder, private Co. E, 153 Ill. Inf.
D. J. Swartant, Co. A, 10th N. Y. Heavy Art.
Andrew Bond.
Daniel Rood, Mexican Soldier.
Wm. Maxton, Sergt. Co. K, 39th Ill. Inf.
Daniel L. Wilson, private Co. D, 26th Iowa Inf.
James Ellis, Jr., Capt. Co. K, 2nd U. S. C. Cav.
Wm. J. Porter, Musician Co. G, 104 Ill. Inf.
C. T. Wilson, Lieut. Co. C, 3rd U. S. C. Cav.
Lorenzo Haynes, Lieut. Co. C, 3rd U. S. C. Cav.
Geo. Harder, private Co. E, 36th Ill. Inf.
John D. McKahin, Lieut. Col. 155 Ind. Vol. Inf.
B. M. Butterfield.
Wm. H. Lang, Co. D, 2nd Ill. Art.

GALLOWAY CEMETERY.

John T. Powers, Co. D, 104 Ill.
L. H. Powers, Co. D, 104 Ill.
Martin V. Bates, Co. F, 100 Ohio.
J. H. McConnell, Co. — 100 Ill.
Uriah Persons, Co. F, 53rd Ill.

NICHOLS CEMETERY.

Delozan De Forrest Vincent, Sergt. Co. C, 1st Ill. Art.
James A. Latimer, Sergt. Co. K, 39th Ill.
Marion L. Butterfield, Lieut. Co. K, 39th Ill.

GENERAL U. S. GRANT,

·MAJOR WILLIAM McKINLEY, :.

MENDOTA.

Officers, Past Post Commanders and Members of

C. A. Andrews Post, No. 135,
G. A. R.

MENDOTA, ILL.

Organized April 25, 1882.

OFFICERS.

H. S. Williams..........................Commander
M. D. Palmer.................Sen. Vice Commander
J. H. Servern........ ....Jun. Vice Commander
Leroy Blanchard...........................Chaplain
J. C. Corbus..... .... Surgeon
Hubbard Clink...................... ...Quartermaster
E. J. Tansey..............................Adjutant
Nelson Lewis.....................Officer of the Day
William Crowley.................Officer of the Guard

PAST POST COMMANDERS.

C. J. Yockey,   Hubbard Clink.
R. F. Shipley,   E. J. Tansey.
Joseph W. Edwards,   George Scullen,
M. D. Palmer,   H. S. Williams.

MEMBERS.

Austin, P. J., private Co. 37th Ill. Inf., farmer.
Berry, John, musician Co. A, 16th Iowa Inf., carpenter.
Burnett, L. O., private Co. H, 115th Ill. carpenter.
Bowen, E. A., colonel 52nd Ill. Inf., banker.
Bartlett, Prescott, capt. Co. C, 7th Ill. Cav., farmer.
Blanchard, Leroy, laborer.
Crooker, L. B., capt. Co. 55th Ill., attorney.

Towers Riding Surface Cultivator

The original of its class, all others being inferior imitations. Do not be deceived into buying any of them.

Tower's pulverizer has no equal for preparing a sod bed and for use in place of harrow after corn is planted.

Send for circular to

J. D. Tower & Bro.

Mendota,   -   -   Illinois.

CRANDALL & LADD

Makers of Harness for every purpose and dealers in Horse Goods Generally.

Mendota, - Illinois.

Kreis Bros. old stand

Corbus, J. C., asst. surg. 75th Ill. supt,

Crowley, William, gun boat Mound City, moulder.

Coler, B. F., priva'e Battery G, 1st Pa. Lt. Art., carp.

Clark, H. R., Co. G, 151th Ill., farmer.

Clink, Hubbard, private Co. M, 17th Pa. Cav., blacksmith.

Eby, H. H., private Co. C, 7th Ill. Cav., farmer.

Edwards, J. W., asst. surg. 40th Ill. Inf , M. D.

Engles, Lewis, private Co. K, 104th Ill., farmer.

Engles, Char'es, private Co. - 75th Ill., farmer.

Graham, Morris, private Co. --, farmer.

Lewis, Nelson, private Co. D, 29th U. S. C. T., laborer.

Lewis, Joseph, musician, farmer.

Lehman, A. janitor.

Miligan, Oscar, farmer.

Morehouse, M., Co. — 64th Ill., farmer.

Naughton, William, laborer.

Owen, W. R., private Co. C, 132nd Ill., M. D.

Orris, G. W., private Co. C, 7th Ill. Cav., painter.

Palmer, M. D., private Co. K, 59th Ill., harness maker,

Place, C., farmer.

Richard, Henry, private Co. A, 26th N. Y. Inf., gard .

Riehardt, Peter, priva'e Co. A, 11th Ill., laborer.

Richard, Jacob. private Co. B, 52nd Ill., farmer.

Reed, F. C., private Co. --, 53d Ill., horse dealer.

Shipley, R. F., sergt. Co. C, 44th N. Y. Inf., carpenter.

Scullen, Geo. S., private 8th N. Y. Independent Battery, musician.

Sandusky, Joseph. farmer.

Smith, L. H, boarding house.

Skiles, James, farmer.

Serven, James, agent.

Telo, Chas., private Co. I, 55th Ill., farmer.

Tansey, E, J., private Co. A, 132d Ill., painter.

Williams, H. S., private Co. I. 2nd Minn. Cav., painter.

Union Soldiers Living at Men-
dota,

Not Members of the Local G. A. R. Post.

E. H. Kingery, Lt. Co. C, 115th Ill., veterinary surg.

Geo. M. Hauk, Co. E, 75th Ill.

Henry Loland, Wis. Regt.

William Witkin, 4th Ill. Cav.

A. D. Heagy, Co. E. 106th Pa.

S. C. Garrard, 10th Mo.

Edward Coleman, Mo. Regt.

A. Baker, Co. --, 101th Ill.

Nicholas Smith, Co.   , 104th Ill.

Mathew Birth, 52nd Ill.

P. W. Wilcox, Co. --, 2nd Iowa Cav.

J. Herr.

EDGAR HAPEMAN,

PROPRIETOR

Mendota Lumber Yard.

Dealer in Sash, Doors, Blinds, Posts, Poles
and everything usually kept by a First
Class Lumber Yard.

MENDOTA,   -   -   -   ILL.

Joseph Ertel,

PROPRIETOR OF

THE EAGLE MILLS.

Dealer in Flour and all Kinds of
Feed. Custom Work Prompt-
ly Attended to.

Mendota,   -   -   Ill.

HARVEY MUNDIE,

DEALER IN

AGRICULTURAL IMPLEMENTS,

Farm Machinery, Wagons,
Machine Oils, Axle
Grease, Binding
Twine, &c.

Agent for Chicago U. S. Scale Co.

MENDOTA.   -   -   -   -   ILL.

V. H. HACKETT,

Union Soldiers Buried in Rest-Land Cemetery, Mendota, Ill.

C. A. Andrews, Lt. Col. 55th Ill.

Geo. W. Morey, Co. B, 2nd Ill.

L. B. Hunter, Co. H, 11th Ill. Inf.

Philip Frank, Co. B, 12th Ill. Inf. Died Jan. 8, 1880.

S. F. Blake, Co. C, 103rd Ill.

S. H. Carr.

T. N. Weireman, Co. B, 12th Ill. Inf.

John Fetzer, Co. C, 32nd Ind. Inf. Died Aug. 28th, 1880.

Joseph M. Scullen, Co. K, 118th Ill.

John R. Scullen, Co. K, 110th Ill.

Abram Smith, Co. D, 30th Ill. Inf. Died March 20th, 1880.

Thomas Sunderlain, Co. D, 15th Vet. Reserve Corps.

John A. Cook, Co. C, 104th Ill.

H. L. Smith, capt. Co. E, 37th Ill. Inf.

James S. Porter, Co. C, 7th Ill. Cav.

D. S. Cooly, Co. A, 57th Ill. Inf.

Joseph Neff, Co. B, 12th Ill. Inf.

Clayton Moody.

Albert Jacoby, Co. A, 132nd Ill.

John Walker, 1st N. Y. mounted rifles. Died March 21th, 1869,

Peal Ambler.

Chas. Andrews, Co. A, 132nd Ill. Died March 29th, 1868.

Peter J. Frrest, died Oct 12th, 1871.

Joseph Crooker, Co. E, 31st Ill. Inf. Died March 1st, 1884.

John E. Cole, Co. D, 5th Wis. Died April 4th, 1884.

D. Kilford, 29th U. S. Colored Regt. Died December 18, 1865.

Henry Stevens, Co. H, 1st Pa. Rifles.

James Huffman, Co. C, 104th Ill. Died June 10th, 1885.

George Kidd, Co. E, 45th Ill. Inf.

John Linney, Colored Regt.

James M. Jack, Co. C, 104th Ill. Died May 4th, 1874.

(Soldiers buried near Mendota, Continued.)

Richard T. Hoffman, Co. I, 112th Ill. Died June 10th, 1885.

Martin Hansell, Co. D, 89th Ill. Inf. Died July 13th, 1887.

James Stubbs, Co. D, 55th Ill. Died Dec. 5th 1891.

Sherman Goff, Co. K, 24 h Wis. Inf.

Chas. Price, Regulars.

Cyrus Critzer, Sergt. maj, 2nd Colo. Cav. Died March 14th, 1885.

Chas. Dewey, Co. C, 7th Ill. Cav. Died April 26th, 1890.

Edward M. Kelly, Co. E, 37th Ill.

Henry Clark, Co. H, 131th Ill. Died July 29th, 1892.

Henry B. Aldritch, Co. A, 132d Ill.

Samuel Shause, Co. H, 112d Ill. Died August 23rd, 1887.

Geo. A. Dodge, Co. A, 57th Ill. Died April 19th, 1895.

Thos. Johnson, Co. A, 132nd Ill. Died December. 8th, 1891.

Casper Rudy, Co. B, 12th Ill. Inf. Died April 3rd, 1896.

Jacob Miller, Co. M, 17th Pa. Cav. Died June 22nd, 1896.

Isaac Eckart, Co. C, 7th Ill. Cav. Died September 29th, 1896.

Fulton Gifford, Q. M., 52nd Ill. Inf. Died October 5th, 1898.

GERMAN LUTHERAN CEMETERY.

August Welkish, Co. I, 4th Ill. Cav. Died August 28th 1882.

Joseph Wurley.

William Meisenbaugh, Mexican War. Died in 1899.

GERMAN CATHOLIC CEMETERY.

Henry Engleskesan, Co. A, 57th Ill.

Michael Reigel, Co. A, 44th Ill. Died September 9th, 1899.

Henry Kneck.

Chris Burkhart, Mexican War. Died in 1899.

CATHOLIC CEMETERY.

William Connors, Co. B, 99th N. Y. Inf.

John Norton

Thomas Baker, Co. A, 17th Ill. Cav. Died June 2nd, 1885.

Michael Boyd, Co. I, 55th Ill.

WEISNER CEMETERY.

Abram George, 8th Ill. Cav. Died Dec. 6th 1898.

Medals of Honor.

Robert F. Shipley, of Mendota, Sergt. Co. A, 140th N. Y. Vol., holds a Medal of Honor voted by n Ac of Congress for capturing a rebel flag on April 1st. 1865.

James W. Larrabee, of Meriden, Sergt. Co. I, 55th Ill., holds a Medal of Honor voted by an Act of Congress for volunteering for a forlorn hope in front of Vicksburg, May 22nd, 1863.

Union Soldiers now Living at Lostant.

Chas. J. Beach, Co. H, 20th Ill., justice of the peace.
Miller Barnhart, corp. Co. B, 53rd Ill., coal scales.
William Raney, Co. E, 4th Ill. Cav., drain tile.
James Watt, Co. F, 171st Pa., laborer.
W. G. Wilson, Co. K, 138th Ill., farmer.
M, Grady, Co. F, 10th U. S. Inf., gardener.
C. P. Adams, Co. B, 4th Ill. Cav., mason.
John Skeets, Co. I, 1st U. S. Art., supervisor.
Thomas Foley, Co. A, 86th Ill., farmer.

Union Soldiers now Living at Vermilionville.

Chas. L. West, private Co G. 55th Ill., farmer.
Jacob Worthington, private Co. G, 57th Ill., farmer.
A. H. West, private Henshaw's Battery, farmer.

Union Soldiers Buried in the Hope Lawn Cemetery, Lostant.

W. L. Rable, Co. D, 53rd Pa. Inf. Died January 25th, 1898.
Silas P. Hansom, Co. C, 64th Ill. Died August 5th 1868.
Daniel C. Kistler, Co. E, 94th Ill. Died October 21st, 1864.
S. A. Dean, Co. I. 104th Ill. Died April 5th, 1876.
R. A. Dugan, Co. C, 64th Ill. Died April 11th, 1869.
Hugh Gaheen, Co. I, 11th Ill. Inf. Died June 11th, 1886,
Joseph Ball, Co. C, 64th Ill. Died January 15, 1879,
Henry S. Consall, Co. G, 11th Ill. Cav. Died December 30th, 1876.
S. W. Park, Co. E, 2nd Md. Inf. Died April 15th, 1891.
John Ross, 12th Pa. Cav. Died April 6th, 1866.
Thomas Rabner, Marine Corps. Died June 23rd, 1867.
Abner Boyle. Died March 6th, 1866. Black Hawk War.

Union Soldiers Buried in the Dana Cemetery.

Joseph J. Jackson, corp. Co. E, 4th Ill. Cav.
James Pritchett, capt. Co. B, 7th W. Va. Inf.
John Thorpe, Co. K, 9th Ill. Cav, Died February, 1899.
Judson Knight, Ohio Vol.
A. Sanders, 11th Ill.

EARLVILLE.

Officers, Past Post Commanders and Members of

McCullough Post No. 475, G. A. R.

EARLVILLE, ILL.

Organized August 21st, 1884.

OFFICERS.

H. V. Chase.............................Commander
J. W. Langley.................Sen. Vice Commander
L. W. Winslow ....Jun. Vice Commander
C. E. Miller.................................Chaplain
A. V. B. Phillips..................Officer of the Day
B. D. Simison ....Officer of the Guard
W. M. Phillips.........................Quartermaster
Samuel Lynn...............................Adjutant
—— ——..Surgeon
B. D. Simison.'................ ....Sergt. Major
J. A. McLaughlin............. ....Q. M. Sergeant

PAST POST COMMANDERS.

Joel Carter,	G. A. Phillipps,
J. C. Kelley,	H. V. Chase,
E. T. White,	C. E. Miller,
T. B. Smith,	W. H. Norton,
G. R. Hoadley,	J. W. Langley,
B. D. Simison,	A. V. B. Phillips,

M. J. Dinsmore.

MEMBERS.

Agnew, Charles, corp. Co. C, 117th Ill., livery.
Bagley, L., private Co. E, 13th U. S. Inf., policeman.
Boozel, H. J., private Co. I, 138th Ill., farmer.
Carter, Joel, sergt. Co. I, 4th Ill. Cav., farmer.
Chase, H. V., private Co. E, 4th Ind. Cav., police justice.
Case, J. A., corp. Co. I, 4th Calf. Inf., farmer.
Dinsmore, M. J., private Co. K, 11th Ill. Inf., farmer.
Fluquay, Henry, private Co. D, 4th Ill. Cav., teamster.

(McCullough Post No. 65, Continued.)

Hoadley, Geo. B., private Co. G, 117th Ill., farmer.
Langley, J. W., private Co. D, 53rd Ill., mason.
Lynn, Samuel, sergt. Co. C, 104th Ill., coal dealer.
Lehman, Fred, private Co. I, 4th Ill. Cav., farmer.
Miller, C. E., corp. Co. E, 22nd Iowa Inf., drayman.
Miller, E. L., private Co. I, 4th Ill. Cav., farmer.
McLaughlin, J. A., private Co. D, 53rd Ill., constable.
Norton, W. H., private Co. A, 104 Ill., engineer.
Phillips, J. W., private Co. I, 4th Ill. Cav., mechanic.
Phillips, A. V. B., private Co. D, 23rd Ill. Inf., carpenter.
Phillips, G. A., private Co. I, 4th Ill. Cav., carpenter.
Phillips, W. M., private Co. B, 23rd Ill Inf., farmer.
Simison, B D., Adjutant 23rd Ill. Inf., farmer.
Smith, T. B., private Co. E, 9th Pa. Reserves, section boss.
Tripp, D. E., private Co. H, 4th Ill. Cav., farmer.
Tillman, D. J., Sergt. Co. M, 14th N. Y. Heavy Art., carpenter.
White, E. T., private Co. B, 28th Wis., clerk.
Warren, F. P., Corp. Co. A, 132 Ill., farmer.
Winslow, L. W., Sergt. Co. C, 104 Ill., farmer.
Winslow, W. S., private Co C, 104 Ill., blacksmith.

Union Soldiers now Living at Earlville, Illinois,

Not Members of the Local G. A. R. Post.

J. H. Peterman, Battery F, 1st Pa Art., hotel.
Chas. McCreedy, Sergt. Co. D, 53rd Ill. laborer.
S. W. Farrell, Sergt. Co B, 15th Ohio Inf., laborer.
J. H. Hoadley, private Co I, 4th Ill Cav , retd. farmer.
J. C. Kelley, private Co. E, 13th Ill. Inf., mus. teacher
Chas. Billings, private Co. I, 4th Ill. Cav., farmer.
J. W. Weidner, private Co. I, 4th Ill. Cav., farmer.
H. E. Ranstead, private Co. D, 53rd Ill., mechanic.
Geo. W. Cleveland, private Co. I, 4th Ill. Cav., laborer.
Joseph Alcorn, private Co. C, 147 Ill., retired farmer.
H. D. Yeager, private Co. 5th N Y. Art., painter.
Lewis Knudtson, private Co. K, 138 Ill., farmer.
J. Z. Harding, private Co. E, 52nd Ill., laborer.
Warren H. Norton, Capt. Co. D, 53rd Ill., city atty.
Wm. E. Hapeman, Capt. Co. M, 4th Ill. Cav., lumber
A. P. Wales, Co. K, 7th Ill. Cav., laborer.
D. L. Barnard, Pa. Regt., furniture.
Joseph McLaughlin, Co. D, 53rd Ill., laborer.
Alvin Case, Co. I, 4th Calif. Inf., farmer.

Union Soldiers Buried in Precinct Cemetery, near Earlville.

W. F. Dodge, 2nd Lieut. Co. A, 124 Ill., died Oct. 5, '81.
Peter Ferguson, Co. D, 53rd Ill., died April 1899.
S. F. Harding, Co. B, 88th Ill., died Sept 30, 1894.
Solan Hill, Co. D, 53rd Ill., died September 1898.
R. O. Dupee, Co. F, 17th Mass., died Feb. 24, 1895.
M. D. Phillips., Co. D, 23rd Ill., died June 14, 1891.
E. F. Horton, Corp. Co. I, 13th Wis. Bat., died in 1897,
Reed Avery, Co. K, 7th Ill. Inf.
B. W. Bagley, Co. A, 104 Ill., died July 2, 1898.
Henry H. Hyde, Co. I, 4th Ill. Cav.
Fayette M. Paine, Lieut. Co. G, 17th Maine, also Co. D
    1st Maine Heavy Art, died May 31, 1898.
Davis C. Ballard, died Feb. 16, 1878.
James E. Doane, 53rd Ill., died April 10, 1898.
W. H. Signor, Co. B, 4th Ill. Cav., died May 5, 1868.
Samuel B. Grover, Co. D, 53rd Ill., died Jan. 8, 1863.
J. N. Pool, Co. D, 53rd Ill., died March 23, 1863.
Jonathan Lewis, Co. A, 104. Ill.
S. T. Stilson, 104 Ill., died April 26, 1888.
F. P. Chase, Corp. Co. D, 53rd Ill.
Samuel M. Haslett, Capt. Co. C, 104 Ill.
Alex. M. Sherlock, 104 Ill., died August 16, 1888.
Edward Horton, Wis. Bat., died August 1897.
Abner F. Beale, Co. D, 53rd Ill., died Dec. 18, 1863.

Wm. Bagley, Co. D, 23rd Ill.
John B. Davidson.
S. D. Wicks, died Jan. 14, 1864.
Ross Seely, Co. E, 36th Ill.
Mathias Stiquel, Co. — 104 Ill.
E. W. Grant, Mexican War, died Feb. 24, 1887.
Jesse Van Namee, war of 1812, died March 14, 1887.

CARTER CEMETERY.

Thos. Wilson, Co. I, 4th Ill. Cav., died Jan. 17, 1885.
David Hare, Co. I, 4th Ill. Cav., died March 1862.
Osro Inel, Co. — Ind. Regt.
Samuel McClure, Co. B, 4th Ill. Cav.
John T. Carter, Co. D, 53rd Ill.

Officers, Past Presidents and Members of

McCullaugh W. R. C. No. 59.

EARLVILLE, ILL.

Organized in January 1887.

Candace, Simison......................,.President
Adda Winslow.......................S. V. President
Alice Wales.........................J. V. President
Hannah Stiquel...........................Chaplain
Della Wilson.............................Secretary
Sara Dupee........... ....Treasurer
Sada Ranstead ....Conductor
Mary Wilson..................................Guard
Alice Brewer..........................Asst. Guard
Nellie Lynn.................. ....Asst. Conductor
Ida Tillman.........................1st Color Bearer
Levania Patch.......... ....2nd Color Bearer
Josephine Kelly....................3rd Color Bearer
Alice Smith........................4th Color Bearer

PAST PRESIDENTS.

Ida Tillman.   Josephine Kelley.
            Della Wilson.

MEMBERS.

Ida Tillman.   Mary Wilson.
Lizzie Norton.   Nellie Lynn.
Josephine Kelley.   Candace Simison.
Sara Dupee.   Sada Ranstead.
Della Wilson.   Clara Clark.
Martha Hill.   Mary Langley.
Alice Smith.   Alice Wales.
Phoebe Case.   Rebecca Dodge.
Alice Brewer.   Julia Case.
Annie Hackman.   Mary Dinsmare.
Levania Patch.   Nellie Kennedy.
Sophie Aitkin.   Nancy Powers.

SHERIDAN.

Officers Past Post Commanders and Members of

Clayton Beardsley Post No. 672,
G. A. R.

SHERIDAN, ILLINOIS.

Organized April 17, 1889.

OFFICERS.

Delos Robinson	Commander
Morris Law	S. V. Commander
Samuel Graf	J. V. Commander
Q. A. Wemple	Adjutant
R. W. Bower	Surgeon
Wright Adams	Chaplain
A. Schlaubusch	Quartermaster
C. A. Averill	Officer of the Day
S. M. Covell	Officer of the Guard
Geo. Godwin	Serg't Major
Bergo Thompson	Q. M. Sergeant

PAST POST COMMANDERS.

Delos Robinson.   James Jennings.
Wright Adams.   W. B. Rockwood.
Bergo Thompson.   Amos Robertson.

MEMBERS.

Adams, Wright, Sergt. Co. E, 91st Ill. farmer.
Averill, C. A. private Co. D, 138th Ill. laborer.
Barber, Moses, private Co. H, 11th Ill. Inf., farmer.
Bower, R. W. private Co. H, 7th Ohio Inf., physician.
Benoit, Chas. private Co. D, 23rd Ill. Inf. laborer.
Bagwell, Marshall, private Co. G, 104th Ill. farmer.
Barrows, J. R. private Co. K, 20th Ill. painter.
Covell, S. L. private Co. H, 156th Ill. teamster.
Cottew, Stephen, private Co. E, 89th Ill. farmer.
Fuller, H. W. private Co. C, 88th Ill. land agent.
Freeman, J. A. Asst. Surgeon 104th Ill. physician.
Girolt, John, Corporal Co. H, 1st Mo., light artillery
    farmer.
Graf, Samuel, private Co. I, 58th Ill. farmer.
Godwin, George, private Co. D, 36th Ill. laborer.
Henderson, George, private Co. G, 10th Ind. Infantry
    retired farmer
Hupp, George C. 1st Lieut. Co. K, 8th Ill. Cav. farmer.
Hamilton, W. private Co. C, 3rd U. S. V. R. Corps
    blacksmith

Jennings, James, private Co. K, 20th Ill., retd. farmer.
Law, Morris, private Co. I, 8th Ill. Cav., carpenter.
Moore, Chauncy, private Co. I, 5th Wis. Inf., teamster.
Minigus, Joseph, private Co. K, 8th Ill. Cav., farmer.
Neff, George, Sergt. Co. F. 36th Ill , merchant.
Pettit, J. W., Corp. Co. F, 154 Ill., physician.
Pierce, Abel, Sergt. Co. B, 32nd Iowa, retd. farmer.
Robinson, Delos, Sergt. Co. C, 129 Ill., merchant.
Rowe, James L., Sergt. Co. G, 104 Ill., retd. farmer.
Rowe, E. M., private Co L, 15th Ill. Cav, retd. farmer.
Robertson, Amos, Corp. Co. D, 116 Ill., painter.
Rockwood, W. B., private Co. K, 20th Ill., carpenter.
Richardson, J. W., private Co. F, 141 Ill , carpenter.
Schlambusch, A., Sergt. Co. A, 15th Wis. Inf. merchant.
Smith, O. H., private Co. D, 18th Ind., J. P.
Solvin, Avin, private Co. G, 53rd Ill., carpenter.
Sears, John, private Co C, 59th Ill., retired farmer.
Snyder, John, private Co. E, 8th Mo. Inf., laborer.
Stearns, I. N., Sergt. Co. D, 75th Ill., merchant.
Thompson, Berge, Sergt. Co. F, 36th Ill., assessor.
Thompson, John, privateCo F, 36th Ill., farmer.
Wemple, Q. A., private Co. I, 141 Ill., farmer.
Warren, W. P., private Co. A, 47th Ill., farmer.

Union Soldiers Buried in Sheridan Cemetery, Mission Township.

Adam Emig, Co. D, 127 Pa., died March 11, 1891.
Robert, Candit, Co. H, 129 Ill.
Geo. W. Sprague, died August 17, 1871.
Clayton Beardsley, died February 23, 1889.
Goodman Olson, Co. D, 3rd Mo. Inf., died July 26, 1891.
Charles Whitney, 10th Mich. Cav.
A. Eastwood, Indian War.

NORWAY CEMETERY.

Ole A. Nelson, Co. F, 141 Ill., died January 15, 1895.
T. Schlambusch, Co. H, 10th Ill. Inf., died July 27, 1893.

SPRADLING CEMETERY.

John Spradling, 11th Ill.
S. C. Barber.
John Spradling, war of 1812.

BAKER'S CEMETERY, NORTHVILLE TOWNSHIP.

James Cottew.

Clayton Beardsley W. R. C., No. 84.

Organized April, 1897.

SHERIDAN, ILLINOIS.

OFFICERS.

Etta L. Law	President
Celia M. Weston	S. V. President
Eliza Robinson	J. V. President
Emily J. Adams	Secretary
Grace W. Carr	Treasurer
Mary L. Wemple	Chaplain
Emma Marahn	Conductor
Bertha Robinson	Assistant Conductor
Mellissa Rockwood	Guard
Nicolena Schlaubusch	Assistant Guard
Lyde Robertson	1st Color Bearer
Emma C. Weston	2nd Color Bearer
Winnie Kember	3rd Color Bearer
Anna Rowe	4th Color Bearer

PAST PRESIDENT.

Celia A. Beardsley.

MEMBERS.

Celia A. Beardsley	Eva C. Bowen
Mabel J. Heavenhill	Ida B Knapp
Ella L. Law	Mary L. Wemple
Mary Burd	Eliza Robinson
Mellissa Rockwood	Celia M. Weston
Bertha Robinson	Nicoline Schlaubush
Jennie Rohne	Julia Grof
Caroline C. Bower	Emily J. Adams
Sarah S. Hibbard	Lyde Robertson
Georgiana Bernard	Anna Rowe
Rose B. Miller	Ella R. Miller
Harriet Hurlburt	Mate E. Soule
Emma Movahn	Lydia Hoffman
Marie E. Wemple	Winnie Kember
Maggie Lewis	Pennelia Fowler
Cava Van Buskirk	Mary L. Ballov
Addie F. Pluess	Grace W. Carr
Irene Scoggin	Sarah Emig
Jennie M. Smith	Emma E. Weston

SENECA.

Officers, Past Post Commanders and Members of

Seneca Post No. 324, G. A. R.

SENECA, ILL.,

OFFICERS.

T. J. Woods...........................Commander
Alexander Hurin..................S. V. Commander
Thomas Cuddingan...............J. V. Commander
C. N. Ralph...................................Chaplain
C. H. R. Thomas.....................Quartermaster
Daniel Smith......... ....Adjutant
Frank Clifford.....................Officer of the Day
Nathaniel Cole.. ....Officer of the Guard
J. W. Ellis........................... ....Q. M. Sergeant
Aaron Fry..........................Sergeant Major

PAST POST COMMANDERS.

F. M. Robinson   George W. Raymond
Samuel Burwell   J. W. Ellis
C. H. R. Thomas   C. N. Ralph
                 T. J. Woods

MEMBERS.

Baker, Nathaniel, Co. A, 104th Ill. farmer.
Battis, William, Co. B, 154th Ill., farmer.
Clifford, Frank, Co. K, 20th Ill., invalid.
Cole, Nathaniel, Co. A, 9th Kansas Cav. farmer.
Cuddingan, Thomas, Co. C, 88th Ill., farmer.
Ellis, J. W. Sergt. Major, 36th Ill., hardware.
Everhart, J. S. Co. I, 97th Pa., wagon maker.
Fischer, Chas. F, Co. I, 36th Ill., invalid.
Fry, Aaron, B. Co. F, 9th Ill. Cav. farmer.
Graves, P. H. Co. A, 88th Ill., retired farmer.
Hurin, Alexander, Co. D, 104th Ill., laborer.
Lammey, Thos. L. Co. L, 15th Ill. Cav. invalid.
Lockwood, Shobal, Co. A, 53rd Ill., laborer.

Meagher, John, Co. K, 39, Ill., R. R. employ.
Mossman, Frank, A, Co. 36th Ill. farmer.
Ralph, Chas. N, Co. I, 36th Ill., farmer.
Raymond, Geo. W. Capt. Co. F, 1st Ark, Inf. retired
    farmer.
Smith, Daniel, Q. M. Sergt. 3rd Wis. Cav. laborer.
Thomas, C. H. R. Co. A, 53rd Ill. attorney.
Woods, Thos. J. Co. I, 164th N. Y. laborer.

Union Soldiers Buried in the Seneca Cemetery.

Samuel Burwell, Lt. Co. B, 10th Minn. died in 1889.
D. H. Underhill, Co. A, 2nd Iowa Inf.
R. A. McFarland, Co. E, 91st Ill.
Hugh McCann, Co. D, 127th Ill.

RANSOM.

Officers, Past Post Commanders and Members of

Francis M. Lane Post No. 247, G. A. R.

RANSOM, ILLINOIS.

Organized May 17th, 1883.

OFFICERS.

Robert Linfor...........................Commander
S. Cleal.....................Senior Vice Commander
A. S. Wilkinson..............Junior Vice Commander
George Cleal........... ....Chaplain
M. J. Lane......................Officer of the Day
W. H. McIntyre..........................Adjutant
R. S. Smalley.......................Quartermaster
John Linfor................. ...Officer of the Guard

PAST POST COMMANDERS.

A. S. Wilkinson,	M. J. Lane,
R. S. Smalley,	W. H. Conard,
George Cleal,	J. C. Deegan,
Robert Linfor,	W. H. McIntyre,
J. G. Newell.	

MEMBERS.

Bradish, C. A., private Co. B, 104 Ill., farmer.
Cleal, George, Corp. Co. H, 127 Ill., farmer.
Cleal, S., private Co. D, 127 Ill., Butcher.
Conard, W. H., Sergt. Co. F, 104 Ill., farmer.
Deegan, J. C., Corp. Co. G, 104 Ill., farmer.
Lane, M. J., private Co. D, 104 Ill., farmer.
Linfor, John, private Co. E, 26th Ill. Inf., farmer.
Linfor, Robert, private Co. C, 1st Ill. Light Art., farmer.
McIntyre, W. H., Sergt. Co. C, 1st Ill. Art., farmer.
Newell, J. G., private Co. E, 104 Ill., farmer.
Ralf, Patrick, private Co. D, 1st Minn. Inf., farmer.
Smalley, R. S., private Co. D, 104 Ill., farmer.
Salsberger, Fred , Sergt. Co. A, 4th Ill. Cav , farmer.
Whitmore, Charles, private Co. G, 1st U. S. Eng., mer.
Wilkinson, A, S., Lieut. Co. B, 8th Mich. Cav., Horseman
Weldon, John, private Co. I, 55th Ill. Inf., farmer.

Not Members of the Local G. A. R. Post.
J. C. Whitmore, private Co. M, 11th Ill. Cav., merchant.
William McCormick, private Co. D, 104 Ill. retd. farmer
J. E. Taylor, 2nd Lieut. Co. G, 4th Mo. Inf., minister.
Charles Higbee, Co. A, 134 Ohio.

JACOB HAGI,

DEALER IN

LIGHT and HEAVY HARDWARE,

Lumber, Lath, Shingles,
Lime, Hair,
Cement, Paints
Oils, Glass.

Farm Implements, Furniture and Undertaking.

All Orders Promptly Filled.

RANSOM, - ILLINOIS.

G. E. SHACKELTON,
DEALER IN

General Merchandise.

Good Fresh and Salt Meats in our
Meat Department. Ice Cream and
Soda in Season.

RANSOM, - ILL.

W. H. Sulzberger & Co.,

MEAT MARKET,

General Merchandise and Hardware.

RANSOM, - ILL.

Officers, Past Presidents and Members of

Francis M. Lane W. R. C., No. 196.

RANSOM, ILLINOIS.

Organized January 21st, 1892.

OFFICERS.

Hattie Wright..............................President
Susan Bradish.................Senior Vice President
Vicie Wilkinson...............Junior Vice President
Bessie Whitmore.........................Secretary
Jannet Cleal.............................Treasurer
Cora Baker................................Chaplain
Nellie Mulvihill.........................Conductor
Sallie Higbee................................Guard
Alice Linfor....................Assistant Conductor
Sophia Hagi.......................Assistant Guard
Jennie McIntyre....................1st Color Bearer
Alice Linfor.......................2nd Color Bearer
Tillie Steven......................3rd Color Bearer
Ella Lindsay......................4th Color Bearer

PAST PRESIDENTS.

Mary Whitmore,   Francis E. Barnes,
Jannet Cleal,   Alice Linfor,
              Jennie McIntyre.

MEMBERS.

Susan Bradish,   Lizzie McCann,
Olive Bower,   Jennie McIntyre,
Cora Baker,   Elma McMichael,
Jannet Cleal,   Nellie Mulvihill,
Julia Cleal,   Anna Newell,
Anna Cunningham,   Theresa Richards,
Sallie Higbee,   Tillie Steven,
Sophia Hagi,   Mrs. Albertina Sulzberger,
Minnie Hagi.   Miss Albertina Sulzberger,
Alice Linfor,   Louise Smalley,
Sophia Lindsay,   Minnie Smalley,
Etta Lindsay,   Hattie Wright,
Ella Lindsay,   Mary Whitmore,
Martha Linfor,   Bessie Whitmore,
Allie Linfor,   Vicie Wilkinson,
              Lizzie Waruement.

Officers, Past Camp Captains and Members of

Gen. Geo. H. Thomas Camp, No. 110, S. of V.

RANSOM, ILLINOIS.

Organized July 22nd, 1887.

OFFICERS.

C. A. Rinker...............................Captain
R. C. Lane...................... ....1st Lieutenant
George Whitmore....................2nd Lieutenant
Pearl Higbee..............................Chaplain

PAST CAPTAINS.

John Blair,	W. H. Whitmore,
O. W. Patton,	L. F. Higbee,
Walter Smalley,	C. W. Bradish.

George S. Bower, Past Surgeon Ill. Div. S. of V.

MEMBERS.

Brown, J. H.,	Kline, Louis.
Cooper, John,	Kline, George,
Conard, D. C.,	Linfor, John,
Conard, Reno,	McCann, D. J.,
Gatchell, Albert,	McIntyre, B. H.,
Harber, Arthur,	McIntyre, R. H.,
Harber, Walter,	Otstot, William,
Hinds, W. A.,	Salsburger, John,
Hilderson, A.,	Stroble, Otto,
Smalley, W. J.	

TONICA.

Officers, Past Post Commanders and Members of

Randolph Post No. 93, G. A. R.

TONICA, ILLINOIS.

Organized March 28th, 1881.

OFFICERS.

A. G. Robinson..........................Commander
A. J. Ebner................ ....Senior Vice Commander
S. W. Burgess................Junior Vice Commander
Thomas Bittle............................Surgeon
A. Trask...............................Chaplain
John Skeets............................Adjutant
B. Ford..........................Officer of the Day
S. Underhill........................Quartermaster
A. Neil........................Officer of the Guard

PAST POST COMMANDERS.

E. E. Hammer.   E. Baldwin,
S. L. B. Black,   Byron Ford,
M. P. Scott,   A. Neil,
Charles Miller,   S. Underhill,
G. W. Howe,   John Skeets,
          A. G. Robinson.

MEMBERS.

Baldwin, E., Corp. Co. A, 88th Ill., painter.
Bush, J. B., Corp. Co. F, 122 Ohio farmer.
Bittle, Thos., private Co. C, 1st Ill. Art., Mason.
Burgess, S. W., private Co. B, 104 Ill., farmer.
Barr, H., private Co. A, 88th Ill., P. M.

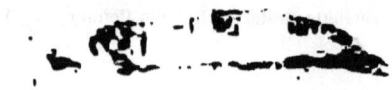

The Amsler Hardware Co.,

Stoves and Tinware.

TONICA,   ·   ·   ·   ILL.

W. E. KREIDER.
GRAIN DEALER.

Coal, Salt, Lime, Cement, Brick, Stone,
and Sand.

TONICA,   –   –   –   ILL,

H, F. & G. W. HARTENBOWER,

Threshers, Engines, Farm Implements.

TONICA,   ·   ·   ILL.

HENRY GUNN.   BERT GUNN.

GUNN & GUNN,
Lawyers,

TONICA,   ·   ·   ILL..

E. F. LAMBERT,

Dealer in Lumber, Lath, Shingles, Sash, Doors, Blinds,
etc. Also agent for Rickard's Steel Lawn Fence
and Eureka Tubular Farm Gate.

TONICA,   ·   ·   ILL.

W. W. HUXTABLE,

Artistic Horseshoer
and General Blacksmith.

Agent for Cooper & Dunlap Buggies,

TONICA,   ·   ·   ·   ILL.

BERT BALDWIN,

Dealer in Fine Cigars, Tobacco and Confectionery. Agent for La Salle Steam
Laundry. Boots and Shoes Neatly
Repaired by William Baldwin.

TONICA,   ·   ·   ILL,

A, J. ZENOR,
DEALER IN

Pure Cream and Milk,

Delivered to all parts of the city.

TONICA,   ·   ·   ·   ·   ILLINOIS.

Ebner, A. J., Sergt. Co. C, 44th Ill., retired farmer.
Ebner, J. F., private Co. A, 49th Pa., farmer.
Ford, B., private Co. A, 88th Ill., farmer.
Grady, M., private Co. H, 10th U. S. Inf., farmer.
How, G. W., Capt. Co. B, 104 Ill., farmer.
Hall, S. A., private Co. I, 11th Ill. Inf., postmaster.
Miller, C., private Co. C, 64th Ill., horsedealer.
Reynolds, R., private Co. C, 1st Ill. Art., farmer.
Robinson, A. G., private Co. B, 104 Ill., farmer.
Richey, D., Corp. Co. H, 129 Ill., potter.
Skeets, John, private 1st U. S. Art., farmer.
Shannon, John, private Co. C, 8th Ohio, laborer.
Smith, F. W., Sergt. Co. G, 55th Ill., farmer.
Smith, H. B., private Co. E, 104, farmer.
Trask, A, private Co. E, 52nd Mass., farmer.
Underhill, S., private Co. A, 88th Ill., gardener.
Walcott, E., private Co. G, 92nd N. Y., carpenter.

Union Soldiers Living at Tonica,

Not Members of the Local G. A. R. Post.

A. B. Bumgarner, Sergt. Co. B, 53rd Ill., laborer.
M. Waite, gardener.
Samuel Landers, Pa. Regt., teamster.
E. S. Ward, private E, 26th Ill., farmer.

John Sherman Camp No. 63, S. of V., was organized at Tonica, in October 1886, but is not now active. Henry B. Ebner was the Captain.

- - PERRY HOUSE. - -

JAMES. A LAMBERT, PROP.

Transient's Home.
Newly Furnished Throughout,

$1.50 per Day.

SPECIAL RATES.

One Block North of Postoffice.

TONICA,   -   -   ILLINOIS.

M. MEEHAN,

Contractor and Builder.

Estimates and plans furnished when desired. Good
work guaranteed. Eighteen years experience.

TONICA,   -   -   **ILLINOIS.**

S. A. HALL, P. M.

*Subscriptions taken for Newspapers
and Magazines.*

TONICA, - - *ILLINOIS.*

Union Soldiers Buried at Tonica,

George Mudge, Co. -- 104 Pa.

Lewis W. Norris, Co. B, 104 Ill.

James B. Snedaker.

S. W. Allen, Co. A, 88th Ill.

M. M. Randolph, Lieut Co. B, 104 Ill., died in 1862.

H. W. Robinson, Co. B, 104 Ill.

H. H. Weld.

John Shepherd, Adjt. 14th Ky.

Alex. McPherson, Co. H, 20th Ill., died Dec. 1862.

Enoch Keller, Co. B, 104 Ill.

Cornelius Leinger. Co. I, 11th Ill. Cav., died in 1862.

Lycergus Wilcoxon.

James E. Barber, Co. A, 88th Ill., died in 1864.

Alvin M. Knapp, Co. E, 50th Ill.

John H. Morley, Co. I, 104 Ill.

J. B. Bullock, Co. A, 88th Ill.

John B. Barrass, Co. I, 12th Ill. Inf.

Champlin R. Potter.

J. W. Alvord Co. K, 11th Ill. Inf.

Alfred Curtis, Co. B, 104 Ill.

Henry W. Underhill, Co. A,19th Ohio Inf.,died in 1864.

Henry G. Graves, Co. B, 104 Ill.

Albert Jones.

E. E. Hamer, U. S. Marine Art., died April 10, 1887.

Wm. McClary.

Augustus Simmons, Co. F, 6th N. Y. Heavy Art.

H. F. Dodge, Co. F, 53rd Ill.

Freeman Nickerson, U. S. Marine Art.

A. Neil, Co. H, 20th Ill., died May 15, 1899.

Union Soldiers Buried in the Allen Cemetery, Near Ransom.

P. N. Webber, Co. A, 1st Ohio Heavy Art., died Dec. 22, 1897.

Ransom Blair, Co. 129 Ill., died March 20, 1898.

E. C. Weyman, Ohio Regt.

John L. Summers.

Elias Lane, war of 1812.

CATHOLIC CEMETERY, RANSOM.

H. F. Jones, Co. C, 8th Mo. Inf., died Sept. 18, 1898.

John Casey, Co. E, 39th Ill., died Jan. 16, 1895.

RUTLAND.

U. S. A.

Officers, Past Post Commanders and Members of

Rutland Post No 292, G. A. R.

RUTLAND, ILLINOIS.

Organized November 18th, 1883.

____

OFFICERS.

John W. Hart.............. ....Commander.
Jonathan Wilson...........Senior Vice Commander
R. L. Dague................Junior Vice Commander
————————...........................Surgeon
William Cholcroft...........'...............Chaplain
John Wadleigh..................... ......Adjutant
Alfred Mateer......................Quartermaster
Henry Nelson....................Officer of the Day
————————.................Officer of the Guard
C. B. Dubois..........................Sergeant Major
————————.....................Q. M. Sergeant

PAST POST COMMAMDERS.

Jonathan Wilson,   John Wadleigh,
Alfred Mateer,   John W. Hart,
    .   John Bailey.

MEMBERS.

Cholcroft, William, private Co. C, 8th Ill. Inf., farmer.
Dubois, C. B., private Co. F, 47th Ill., retired farmer.
Dague, R. L., private Co. I, 15th W. Va. Inf., farmer.
Gray, Robert, private Co. C, 3rd Iowa Inf., farmer.
Hart, John W., private Co. D, 127 Ill., farmer.
Mateer, Alfred, Sergt. Co. A, 47th Ill., J. P.
Nelson, Henry, Co. H, 104 Ill., farmer.
Wilson, Jonathan, private Henshaws Bat., retd. farmer.

JOHN WADLEIGH,
Notary Public, Insurance Agent and Conveyancing.
RUTLAND,   ·   ·   ·   ILL.

C. E. ROHRER,
First Class Barber Shop.
Agent for New Troy Steam Laundry.
RUTLAND,   –   ··   –   ILL.

A. MATEER·
POLICE MAGISTRATE.
Collections Promptly Attended to.
RUTLAND,   ··   –   ILL.

F. G. BLANDIN,
DRUGS, BOOKS, WALL PAPER.
Notary Public.
RUTLAND,   ·   ·   ·   ILL.

THE DAUGHTER OF THE REGIMENT.

Officers, Past Presidents and Members of

Rutland W. R. C. No. 39.

RUTLAND, ILLINOIS.

Organized November 19th, 1895.

OFFICERS.

Angenora D. Thomas......................President
Jennie Golder.................Senior Vice President
Jeanette Proctor. ....Junior Vice President
Mary C. Brevoart...........................Treasurer
Stella Willoughby..........................Secretary
Georgia Coons...............................Chaplain
Ida Lutton.................................Conductor
Addie Hoskins..................................Guard
Francis Rowland... ....Assistant Conductor
Ella Sutton....... ....Assistant Guard
Nettie Rohrer......................1st Color Bearer
Eva Stout...... .. ..2nd Color Bearer
Lou Chamberlain..................3rd Color Bearer
Laura Mullin......................4th Color Bearer

PAST PRESIDENTS.

Adelia Ingram,   Eva Stout.

MEMBERS.

Pauline Wadleigh,   Lou Chamberlain,
Nettie Rohrer,   Mary C. Brevoart,
Bertha Ensign,   Addie Romire,
Eva Stout,   Georgia Coons,
Ida Lutton,   A. M. Hart,

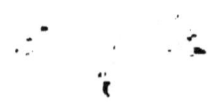

[Rutland W. R. C. No. 39, Continued.]

Stella Willoughby,
Francis Rowland,
Jeanette Proctor,
Mary J. Nelson,
Laura Mullen,
Cora Bane,
Angenora D. Thomas,
Ella Sutton,
Mayma Ingram,
Addie Hoskins,
Jennie Golder,

Elvina Jackson,
Sarah Gray,
Mary C. Howell,
Sarah M. Ensign,
Sylvia M. Dolen,
Hattie Davison,
Mary Webber,
Fannie T. Roe,
Mary S. Winans,
Miriam Miller,
Adelia Ingram.

Elbridge Chapman Camp No. 311, S. of V., was organized at Rutland in February 1890, but is not now active. Past Captains, William E. Stout and William H. Wudleigh.

Union Soldiers living at Rutland.

Not Members of the Local G. A. R. Post.

William O. Ensign, Corp. 11th Ohio Indp. Bat.
Asa Dunham.

Union Soldiers Buried at Rutland.

George W. Williamson, Co. D,77th Ill., died Jan. 22, '66.
Edward N. Benton, died January 26, 1866.
Robert Bird, Co. D, 8 h Ill. Vol Inf.
Freeman A. McPherson, died May 1, 1870.
Justin Moore, Co. B, 33rd Ill., died December 18, 1865.
Lorenzo G. Stout, Co. I, 104 Ill., died January 13, 1893.
Egbert S. Dresser, Co. H, 104 Ill., died Nov. 30, 1895
William McDonald, Co. I, 104 Ill.
Harry S. Whipple,
Enoch Thomas, Black Hawk War.

BELROSE CEMETERY.

William Bigford, Co. H, 7th Wis. Cav., died Mar. 9, '02.
Henry Selar, Cogswells Battery, died in 1880.
John Parrot, Co E, 53rd Ill. Inf.
John Gibson 1st Pa. Inf. war of 1812.
Julius Ulrich, Black Hawk War.

DANIELS CEMETERY.

George Spencer, Capt. Battery C, 1st Ill. Art.
Henry Howe, Battery C, 1st Ill. Art.

GRAND RIDGE.

GRAND RIDGE

Union Soldiers Living at Grand Ridge.

Wm. M. Jones, Co. G, 104 Ill., ex-p. m.
James S. Lewis, Co. G, 16th Pa. Cav., physician.
Harvey Snook, Co. F, 11th Ill. Cav., retired farmer.
Geo. W. Hook, 1st Va. Inf., auctioneer.
J. N. Piersell, Co. G, 16th Pa. Cav., retired farmer.
Lacy Hibbs, Co. H, 11th Ill. Inf., farmer.
Ryen Whitehill, Co. L, 2nd W. Va. Cav., laborer.
John J. Ramler, Co. H, 54th Ill., janitor.
John N. Boyd, Co. K, 7th Pa. Cav., engineer.
Scofield Singer. Co. — 53rd Ill., farmer.
Richard Poundstone, Troop L, 15th Ill. Cav., farmer.
John M. Shape, Co. F, 1st Pa. Res. Cav., clerk.
James Anderson, Co. F, 16th Ill., teamster.
George A. Parker, Co. B, 7th Maine Light Inf., mason.
Anton Smith, Co. A, 104 Ill., farmer.
William Shields, Co. C, 11th Ill. Cav., farmer.

Union Soldiers Buried in the Pound-stone Cemetery, Farm Ridge Township,

George Poundstone, Sergt. 53rd Ill., died July 12, 1863.
David Anderson, Co. M, 4th Ill. Cav., died Sept. 6, 1863.
John D. Reese, Co. A, 1st W. Va. Cav., died Feb. 21, '99.

EPISCOPAL CHURCH CEMETERY.

William W. Morgan, Co. D, 2nd Ill. Art.
Jonathan K. Yost.
David Anderson, Lieut. Co. H, 62nd Ill., died Oct. 6, '63

LUTHERAN CEMETERY.

Thos. C. Warren, Co. E, 66th Ohio Inf.

SERENA.

Union Soldiers Living at Serena.

William G. Putney, bugler Battery I, 2nd Ill. Light
Art. Vol., physician.
Justus Carter, Co. D, 23rd Ill., grain dealer.
R. H. Pooler, private 16th Co. 60th Ohio Indpt Sharp
Shooter, hardware.
John Sears, Co. C, 59th Ill., retired farmer.
Isiah W. Kelley, 1st W. Va. Art., laborer.
John McKinley, Co. G, 8th Ill. Inf., mason.
Joseph Nelson, Co. E, 62nd Ohio, farmer.

Union Soldiers Buried in Serena Cemetery.

Josiah Bagley, Corp. Co. C, 1st Ill. Light Art., died July
27, 1898.
George Campbell, Co. B, 53rd Ill., died April 10, 1887.
Chas. Roger, Co. 101 Ill., died July 29, 1861.
Henry Hoxey, Co. E, 26th Ill.
P. Peterson, Co. C, 1st Ill. Art.
C. P. Chase, Co. 1st Wis.

Spanish-American War Sol diers.

Not Including Members of the Ottawa and Streator Companies.

Charles Fischer, Corp. Co K, 6th Ill. Inf. Mendota.
Leroy Kingery, Corp. Co. K, 6th Ill. Inf. Mendota.
Henry Kuhl, private Co. K, 6th Ill. Inf. Mendota.
Harvey Powell, private Co. K, 6th Ill Inf. Mendota.
Charles Gagstetter, private Co. K, 6th Ill. Inf, Mendota.
George Clarkson, private Co. K, 6th Ill. Inf. Mendota.
Roy Girard, private Co. K, 6th Ill. Inf. Mendota.
Jay Girard, private Co. K, 6th Ill. Inf. Mendota.
Carl Pross, private Co. K, 6th Ill. Inf. Mendota.
William McCabe, private Co. K, 6th Ill. Inf. Mendota.
George Mays, private Co. K, 6th Ill. Inf. Mendota.
Clarence Huck, private Co. K, 6th Ill. Inf. Mendota.
Edward Riegel, private Co. K, 6th Ill. Inf. Mendota.
Mark Hurlburt, private Co. K, 6th Ill. Inf. Mendota.
John Brennan, private Co. K, 6th Ill. Inf. Mendota.
Lawrence Prescott, Corp. Co. E, 6th Ill. Inf. Mendota.
Leo A. Stevens, private Co. I, 12th U. S. Inf. LaSalle.
Horace Dunn, private Co. I, 12th U. S. Inf. LaSalle.
Edward Shaw, Corp. Co. I, 1st Ill. Cav. LaSalle.
John Gardner, private Co. I, 12th U. S. Inf. LaSalle.
Adolph Eastman, private Co. I, 12th U. S. Inf. LaSalle.
Abel Newton, private Co. I, 1st Mo. Inf. LaSalle.
George McGann, private Co. I, 1st Mo. Inf. LaSalle.
Harry Hassett, Co. G, 6th Ill. Inf, LaSalle.
James McClaud, Co. B, 6th Ill. Inf. LaSalle.
William Gardner, Co. B, 6th Ill. Inf.
Edward McGlouchlin, Co. 6th Ill. Inf.
Clarence Dick, Co. 1st Ill. Cav. LaSalle.
C. C. Peterman, 12th U. S. Inf. b and Earlville.
Jason M. Farrar Sergt. Co I, 12th U. S. Inf. Earlville.
Dell Cox, Co 1st Ill Inf. Earlville.
Lester Davis, Co. I, 3rd Ill. Inf. Earlville.
Charles Lehman, private Co. C, 12th U. S. Inf. Earlville.
Abel C. Doughty, private Co. I, 12th U. S. Inf. Earlville

Maj. Gen. William R. Shafter.

Spanish-American War Soldiers Continued

Chas. A. Williams, private Co. F, 1st Ill. Cav. Ottawa,
Chester J. Dick, private Co. F, 1st Ill. Cav. Ottawa,
Edward Wilby, private Co.—12th U. S. Inf. Ottawa.
B. Skinner, private Co.—1st Colo. Inf. Ottawa.
W. F. Banchle, Hosp. Corps Ottawa.
C. J. Zuranzig, Ottawa.
G. A. Lloyd, Ottawa.
Harry Husten, Ottawa.
E. J. Wheeler, Ottawa,
F. E. Bee, Ottawa.
C. Guenther, Corp. Co. I, 12th U. S. Inf. Peru.
F. Schick, Corp. Co. I, 12th U. S. Inf. Peru.
William Franks private Co I, 2nd Ill. Inf. Peru.
C. Aderhold, Co.—1st Ark. Peru.
E. Riegel, Co.—6th Ill. Inf. Peru.
F. E. Rinicki, U. S. Navy Peru.
H. Loeller, Co. I, 12th U. S. Inf. Peru.
L. Lassig, Co. I, 12th U. S. Inf. Peru.
L. Stremver, Co—2nd Neb. Inf. Peru.
Joseph Glass, Co. I, 12th U. S. Inf. Peru.
T. R. Edgerton, private Co. A. 1st Ill. Inf. Tonica.
Henry B, Ebner, Sergt. Co. D, 5th Ill. Inf. Tonica.
Charles Hartenbower, private Co. D, 5th Ill. Inf.
      Tonica.
Geo. Jennings, Co. 5th Ill. Inf, Tonica.
William P. Hoffman, private Co, G, 6th Ill. Inf. Sand-
      wich.
George Law, Co. I, 3rd Ill. Inf. Sandwich.
Charles Worthingham, Marseilles.
Charles Nusbaum, Seneca.
Geo. F. Taylor, Co. B, 12th U. S. Inf. Grand Ridge.
Ralph C. Woodard, Co. B, 12th U. S. Inf. Grand Ridge
H. Bradshaw, Co. H, 9 h Ill. Inf. Lostant.
Zedam Bradshaw, Co. H, 9th Ill. Inf. Lostant.

CAPT. CHARLES D. SIGSBEE.

Carlton Herbert Jencks, of OttawaGunner's Mate, went down with the Maine Feb. 15, 1898, buried in Colon Cemetery Havana.

W. F. Stanley, of Rutland, Corp. Co. E, 2nd U.S.Inf. died Nov. 7, 1898. Buried at Lower, Salem, Ohio.

Samuel Armstrong, Co. I, 12th U. S. Inf. died Oct. 28, 1898. Buried in Columbus Cemetery North Ottawa.

Robert M. Leland, Co. C, 3rd Ill. Vol. Inf. died at Springfield, May 16, 1898. Buried in Ottawa Ave. Cemetery Ottawa.

Edward C. Shuler, Co. C, 3rd Ill. Vol. Inf. died at Chickamauga Park June 16, 1898. Buried in Ottawa Ave. Cemetery Ottawa.

Otto C. Osmunson, Co. C, 3rd Ill. Vol. Inf. died July 27, 1898, at Fort Monroe, Va., Buried in Brum back Cemetery near Danway.

Marcus E. Osmunson Co. C, 3rd Ill. Vol. Inf. died April 1899. Buried in Brumback Cemetery near Danway.

Irving R. Campbell, Corp. Co. C, 3rd Ill. Vol. Inf. died Aug. 14, 1898. Buried at sea.

John A. Smith, Co. C, 3rd Ill. Vol. Inf. died at Porto Rico Aug. 20, 1898. Buried at Mendota.

Albert P. McCoy, Co. C, 3rd Ill. Vol. Inf. died at Guayama, Porto Rico, Oct. 7, 1898. Buried at Henry, Ill.

William H. Krause, Co. C, 3rd Ill. Vol. Inf. died Nov. 15, 1898. Buried at Summit View Ottawa.

George C Vincent, Co. C, 3rd Ill. Vol. Inf. musician, died April 1899. Buried at Marseilles.

Frank B. Killifer, Sergt. Co. A, 3rd Ill. Vol. Inf. Buried at Streator.

Claude W. Peters, Corp. Co. A, 3rd Ill. Vol. Inf. died at Porto Rico, Aug. 23, 1898. Buried at Streator.

J. A. Daniels, Co. A, 3rd Ill. Vol. Inf. died at Chickamauga Park, June 8, 1898.

L. Burton Bradish, Corp. Co. A, 3rd Ill. Vol. Inf. died off the coast of Porto Rico Oct. 23, 1898. Buried at Mayaguez, Porto Rico.

ROSTER OF SURVIVORS
53rd Regt. Illinois Vet. Vol. Inf.

Organized at Ottawa, October 1861. Mustered out of service July 1865.

Colonel J. W. McClanahan, Sparland, Illinois.
Colonel R. H. McFadden, Mattoon, Illinois.
Lieut. Colonel C. H. Brush, Campbell, Minnesota.
Major T. C. Gibson, Ottawa, Illinois.
Major E. H. Stumph, Ottawa, Illinois.
Surgeon W. W. Welsh, Galesburg, Illinois.
Surgeon J. O. Harris, Ottawa, Illinois.
Surgeon Henry Zeising, Peru, Illinois.
Surgeon J. F. Williams, 127 Centre St., Chicago, Ill.
Chaplain P. P. Cleveland, Rogers Park, Illinois.
Chaplain F. J. Crawford, Chicago Illinois.

COMPANY A.

Armstrong, Wm., Captain, Pueblo, Colorado.
Baird, Thomas W., Hopperville, Kansas.
Boyd, Michael, Chicago, Illinois.
Coarting, Thomas L., Burdette, Missouri.
Collins, James A , 175 Wisconsin St., Milwaukee, Wis.
Doyle, Michael, Osage City, Kansas.
Fitzgerald, John, Yorkville, Illinois.
Graham, Wm. F, Ottawa, Illinois.
Holmes, Henry, Ottawa, Illinois.
Herbert, Patrick, Ransom, Illinois.
Hilderbrand, S. G., Lincoln, Nebraska.
Hamilton, William B., Sunbury, Illinois.
Herschell, Fred, Monfield, Illinois.
Jennings, F. A , Dunlap, Iowa.
Jones, Frank C., Marseilles, Illinois.
Kelly, W. A., Streator, Illinois.
Keeler, Dennis, ---- California.
Lockwood, S , Morris, Illinois.
Miller, H. J., Dewitt, Illinois.
McCashland, J. R., Fairmont, Nebraska.
Nettleton, G. C , Odell, Illinois.
Norton, Zina, Hastings, Nebraska.
O'Leary, Michael, Indianola, White Willow Co., Neb.
O'Leary, John, Shales, Iowa.

(Company A, 53rd Ill. Inf., Continued.)

Reeder, J. J., LaSalle, Illinois.
Randall, Henry C., Morris, Illinois.
Renne, Watson, Marseilles, Illinois.
Renne, James, Eagle Grove, Iowa.
Smith, William, Jules City, Kansas.
Sigler, R. D., Seneca, Illinois.
Thomas, C. H. R., Seneca, Illinois.
Woodberry, O. A., Hansen, Nebraska.
Wyman, Henry, South Ottawa, Illinois.
Wood, John G., Omaha, Nebraska.
Yarnell, John F., Winnamac, Indiana.
Zellers, Jacob, Ottawa, Illinois.

COMPANY B.

Brunk, William, Clarkes, Nebraska.
Beckwith, Dan., Ottawa, Illinois.
Bumgarner, A. B., Tonica, Illinois.
Barnhart, Miller, Lostant, Illinois.
Brewster, Frank, 1138 Parelle St., Atchison, Kansas.
Baxter, R. A., Hurley, Wisconsin.
Cuningham, E. V., Valparaiso, Nebraska.
Clarkes, A. W. Columbus, Missouri.
Cole, Lyman N., —— Missouri.
Davis, H. M., Wapello, Iowa.
Disnay, Joseph, Coffeyville, Kansas.
Frary, Frank, Galesburg, Illinois.
Frary, Charles, Moline, Illinois.
Galloway, James, East Chicago, Indiana.
Gardner, M. H., Joliet, Illinois.
Harper, Samuel, Gardner, Illinois.
Haney, Clark B., Elkhorn, Indiana.
Jones, Thomas H., Joliet, Illinois.
Kennedy, Lieut. H. Roseville, Illinois.
Looney, William, White Sulphur Springs, Montana.
Mooney, David, Burier City, Kansas.
Minard, Henry, Grand Ridge, Illinois.
Montgomery, James, Eskridge, Kansas.
McKay, A. B., Longtown, Kansas.
Newton, A., Lamar, Missouri.
Pool, Gilvary, Morris, Illinois.
Plauffe, Jacob, Blairstown, Iowa.
Ready, Jesse, Nebraska City, Nebraska.
Specie, Gilbert, Morris, Illinois.
Trenary, James, Arkansa City, Kansas.
Watson, William H., Chebanse, Illinois.
Yockey, Charles J., Ottawa, Illinois.

COMPANY C.

Able, Charles, Fremont, Nebraska.
Brooks, Louis, 5826 Wentworth St., Englewood, Ill.
Drake, J. H., Ottawa, Illinois.
Grant, O. B., Marseilles, Illinois.
Haynes, James H., Cornell, Illinois.
Horner, John W., S.Ottawa, Illinois.
Hall, O. A., Ord, Nebraska.
Harris, J. W., Chicago, Illinois.
Huttis, Eber, Marseilles, Illinois.

(Company C, 53rd Ill. Inf., Continued.)

Jones, Patrick, Devitt. Nebraska.
King, F. G., Captain, Ottawa, Illinois.
Kinberlin, S. B., Farragut, Iowa.
Mullen, John W., Lafayette, Indiana.
Olsen, Barney, Marseilles, Illinois.
Philmore, William, S. Ottawa, Illinois.
Read, Henry, Chicago, Illinois.
Skinner, R. E., S. Ottawa, Illinois.
Singer, E. S., Grand Ridge, Illinois.
Strand, O. C., Ottawa, Illinois.
Todd, David H., Ottawa, Illinois.

COMPANY D.

Agnew, Frank, Sailesbury, Missouri.
Austin, Herbert, Newtonia, Missouri.
Cameron, A. A. Hebron, Nebraska.
Firkins, William, East Paw Paw, Illinois.
Flick, Michael, Streator, Illinois.
Herron, J. M., Freedom, Illinois.
Kingslow, A. S., Sycamore, Illinois.
Larkins, Lot C., Cabery, Illinois.
McReedy, Charles, Earlville, Illinois.
McLaughlin, J. A., Earlville, Illinois.
McLaughlin, Joseph K., Earlville, Illinois.
Norton, W. H., Captain, Earlville, Illinois.
Plank, L. A., Carlsch, Illinois.
Pine, R. D., Ashland, Nebraska.
Rockabrand, Charles, Clinton, Iowa.
Rupert, R. W. Blandinsville, Illinois.
Ranstead, Herbert E. Earlville, Illinois.
Streetor, W. F., Earlville, Illinois.
Tracey, George, Morris, Illinois.
Temple, Thomas S., 3705 Ellsworth Ave., Chicago, Ill.
Wincent, James, Atlantic, Iowa.

COMPANY E.

Basset, W., Captain, Peoria, Illinois.
Bornean, David, Manteno, Illinois.
Campbell, A. H., Webber, Nebraska.
Goff, I. N., Webber, Nebraska.
Griffin, John A., Danville, Illinois.
Miles, Joseph A., Louisville, Kentucky.
Palmer, William H., Blair, Nebraska.
Piatt, Samuel, Walden, Illinois.
Tuson, H. C, York, Nebraska.
Vaugh, Mrs. Charles M., Chebanse, Illinois.
Weller, N. J., La Salle, Illinois.
Wilkinson, G. B., Lincoln, Nebraska.

COMPANY F.

Ashley, Harry., Gibson City, Illinois.
Cox, Spencer J., Seneca, Illinois.
Cland, Prospe, Woolstock, Iowa.
Dodge, H. F., Tonica, Illinois.
Deltz, David, Moline, Illinois.
Earl, William E., Denver, Colorado.
Fabian, Valentine, Lake Station, Indiana.
Harrington, William, Marseilles, Illinois.

Holden, David L., Matteson, Illinois.
Mettles, Rev. A. B., Evanston, Illinois.
Mosher, George I., Oskaloosa, Kansas.
Persons, Uriah, Marseilles, Illinois.
Putman, James, Hulbert Corner, Wisconsin.
Prickingham, F. A., Evans, Illinois.
Palmer, William B., Clifton Hotel, Denver, Colorado.
Potter, John, White Sulphur Springs, Montana.
Sparks, S. J., Marseilles, Ill.
Vorce, Charles H., 20 Michigan Avenue, Chicago, Ill.

COMPANY G,
Colstock, David, Gardner, Illinois.
Clark, C, H., Chicago, Illinois.
Hallett, Charles, 6618 Michigan Ave., Chicago, Ill.
Knickerbocker, Nels, Ottawa, Illinois.
Lodge, George R., 71 Dearborn street, Chicago, Ill.
Solvin, Avin, Norway, Illinois.
Tulton, A., Table Rock, Nebraska.
Wilkson, J., Henry, Illinois.

COMPANY H.
Atwood, Timothy, Chicago, Illinois.
Barton, John, Sparland, Illinois.
Denby, William, Chillicothe, Illinois.
Geiselman, George, Ottumwa, Iowa.
Hunter, Hiram A., Peoria, Illinois.
Hatfield, J. D., Nileigh, Nebraska.
Larson, Thomas, Morris, Illinois.
Matthew, F, Aurora, Illinois.
Neemons, G. J. G., Minonk, Illinois.
Nelson, John, Chillicothe, Illinois.
Rathbun, Alonzo, Columbus, Ohio.
Stone, H. A., Mineral, Illinois.
Thomas, Leyman, Minonk, Illinois.
Temple, Thomas H., 3505 Ellis Ave., Chicago, Ill.
Vincent, James, Atlantic, Iowa.
Worlds, Hiram, Streator, Illinois.

COMPANY I.
Abell, William, Howell, Nebraska.
Armstrong, W. S., Ottawa, Illinois.
Buchanan, J. E., Streator, Illinois.
Cunningham, William, Ottawa, Ill.
Fitzgerald, Thos., Nevada, Illinois.
Gilman, J. R., Valley, Nebraska.
Hallisham, John, Wing, Illinois.
Hefron, E., Emington, Illinois,
Jennings, Henry, Dunlap, Iowa.
Kidd, A. J., 1316 Wilson Ave., Chicago, Illinois.
Kirk, D. W., South Bend, Nebraska.
Kinney, James A., Soldiers' Home, Los Angeles, Cal.
Moss, T. J., Rogers Park, Illinois.
McCausland, B. C., Grafton, Nebraska.
Marblow, H. A., Spring Creek, Nebraska.
McCalla, John, Pontiac, Illinois.
Malloy, James A., Cherokee, Kansas.
Matthews, H, Raymond, Illinois.

Company I 53rd Regt. Ill. Vol. Inf. Continued.

Nelson, Thomas, Norway, Illinois.
Olmstead, P. E., Hammond, Louisiana.
Orr, J. C, Council Bluffs, Iowa.
Richardson, A. A., Williamsburg, Nebraska.
Read, Frank O., Troy Grove, Illinois.
Wing, Charles E., Ottawa, Illinois.

COMPANY K.

Ryan, R. R., Albany, Nebraska.
Sanders, Joseph, La Salle, Illinois.

CAPTAIN FORD'S CAVALRY.

J. L. Marriner, Chicago, Illinois.
Peter Stine, El Paso, Illinois.
Thomas E. Lancy, Seneca, Illinois.
John Barber, Seneca, Illinois.
U. S. Painter, Streator, Ill.
Samuel Porter, Ottawa, Illinois.

ARTILLERY.

Lieut. Wm. Burgess, Ottawa, Ill.
Wm. Cunningham, Ottawa, Ill.
John Fribbs, Ottawa, Ill.
Teddy Ryan, Ottawa, Ill.
Dan'l Tucker, Ottawa, Ill.
L. L McKinley, Ottawa, Ill.

General John A. Logan.

Union Soldiers Buried North Bluff, Ottawa.

W. H. S. Wallace, Col. 11th Ill. Inf. and Brig. Gen.
T. Lyle Dickey, Col. 4th Ill. Cav.
Cyrus Dickey, Lieut. 4th Ill. Cav.

Union Soldiers Buried in South Ottawa and Jewish Cemeteries.

Chas. Collier, Co. E, 4th Ohio Cav. died Dec. 30, 1887.
Maurice Fullerton, Co. C, 1st Ill. Art. died Jan. 5, 1862.
Chas. H. Green, Co. F, 100th Ill. Inf. died March 15, 1873.
Charles Hadstrong, Co. A. 104 Ill. Inf. died May 24, '77.
Geo. N. Chamberlin, Lieut. Co. K, 10th N. Y., Inf. died Jan. 5, 1895.
George Malaby, Co. I, 53rd Ill. Inf. died May 3, 1866.
Henry M. Shaw, Co, E, 26th Ill. Inf. died March 26, '65
Caleb Wixorn, Co. H, 11th Ill. Inf. died Aug. 9, 1875.
John Phillemore, Jr., Co. C, 53rd Ill. Inf. died Nov. 29, 1881.
Richard E. Edgecomb, Co. C, 1st Ill. Art. died June 20, 1885.
Richard E. Edgecomb, Co. K, 64th Ill. Inf. died Jan. 7, 1873.
Wm. P. Farnsworth, Co. B, 2nd Iowa, died Sept. 17, 1865.
Theodore Pickens, Co. I, 11th Ill, Inf. died Dec. 6, '61.
Thos. Cunningham, Lieut. Co. L, 5th N. Y., Cav. died Aug. 3, 1867.
Thos. Jordan. Co. L, 15th Ill. Cav. died Feb. 11, 1873.
David Lathrop, Co. E, 104th Ill. Inf. died Sept. 1863.
Joseph A. Leonard, Co. L, 15th Ill. Cav. died Nov. 23, 1864.
Hugh A. Dummit, Co. A, 59th Ill. Inf. died Oct.6, '76.
Thomas Stump, Host. Steward 53rd Ill. died March 4, 1881.
Wynne Stump, Co. C, 53rd Ill. Inf. died June 8, 1882.
James E. Bronson, Corp. Co. A, 4th Ill. Cav. died July 22, 1883.
Bernard Vesosky, Co. I, 24th Ill. Inf. died Dec. 26, '86.
William Bayne, Sergt. Co. E, 26th Ill. Inf. July 24, '69.
N. W. Beckwith, Co. I, 20th N. Y. Cav. died Dec. 22 1885.
Thomas Cooper, Gunboat Sampson, U. S. N. died Aug. 2, 1889.
Deles W. Graves, Co. C, 8th Ill. Inf. died March 21, '93.
Ira Smith, Co. H, 11th Ill. Inf. died March 16, 1862.
Simon P. Milland, Co. Co. D, 100 Ill. Inf. died Oct. 6, '91.
Jesse Doolittle, Co. C, 53rd Ill. Inf. died Nov. 28, '91.
Walter Singer, Cogswells Battery died March 18, 1898.
Jacob Degan, Co. I, 24th Ill. Inf. died Nov. 27, 1845.
Wm. Degau, 1st Washington D. C. Art. died June 5, '99.

UNION SOLDIERS BURIED IN OTTAWA AVENUE AND
GERMAN CEMETRIES, WEST OTTAWA.

Thomas Barney, Co. I, 11th Ill. Inf. died Oct. 30, 1887.
Douglas Streator, Co. D, 8th Ohio Inf. died Nov. 12, '87.
Peter Wolf, Co. D, 2nd Ill. Art. died Dec. 1, 1887.
John H. Druitt, Co. A, 64th Ill. Inf. died July 15, 1888.
Thos. Beedy, Co. I, 11th Ill. Inf. died March 7, 1889.
Menzo Wagner, Co. M, 4th Ill. Cav.
W. D. Price, Lieut. Co. A, 53rd Ill. Inf. died Oct. 5, '62.
H. E. Price, Sergt. Co. B, 104th Ill died July 20, 1864.
Edward Hays, Co. F, 10th Ill. Inf.
Edward F. Herrick, Lieut. and Q. M. 104th Ill. Inf.
Hiram Prescott, Co. C, 1st Ill. Art. died Oct. 10, 1875.
Napoleon Beanbren, Co. E, 53rd Ill. Inf. died June 7,
     1871.
Henry Fredenburg, Sergt. Cogswells Battery, died July
     17, 1870.
Isaac H. Fredenburg, Co. L, 15th Ill. Cav. died July
     11, 1884.
W. C. Brusk, Co. D, 104th Ill. Inf. died April 13, '63.
W. H. W. Cushman, Col. 53rd Ill. Inf. died Oct. 29, '78.
Thos. S. Bowen, Co. F, 36th Ill. Inf. Died May 15, '76.
Joseph W. Phelps, Co. M, 4th Ill. Cav.
Lyman Potter, Co. A, 104th Ill. Inf.
Hiram F. Higby, capt. Co. L, 15th Ill. Cav. Died in
     1863.
William B. Fyfe, Co. G, 129th Ill. Inf.
Milton Strawn, Lt. Co. E, 104th Ill. Inf. Died Dec.
     22, 1862.
John Meingue, Co. A, 4th Ill. Cav. Died Mar. '62.
A. B. Moore, Col. 104th Ill. Inf. Died June 7, 1879.
A. W. Hollister, lieut. ———
F. D. McIsaves, sergt. Co. H, 11th Ill. Inf. Died Nov.
     25, 1862.
Andrew Anderson, Co. A, 64th Ill. inf. Died Mar. '64.
Charincey Burr, died Feb. 14, 1863.
Henry Hamilton, Co. I, 11th Ill. Inf. Died May 30, '64,
James H. Leland. Died Aug. 18. 1864.
Ferdinand Robinson, Co. C, 4th Iowa. Died May 18,
     1863.
John Collins. Co. K, 90th Ill. Inf. Died Dec. 31, '80.
Wm. Emrich, Co. I, 138th Ill. Inf. Died Nov. 1864.
H. H. Hentz, capt. Co. H, 24th Ill. Inf.
Henry Rose, Co. I, 24th Ill. Inf.
Francis Potter, private Co. A, 104th Ill. Inf.
David Bailey, Co. C, 53rd Ill. Inf. Died Nov. 21, '71.
John H. Doty, capt. Co. E, 104th Ill. Died July 20, '64
Norton Fields, Co. — 104th Ill. Died in 1870.
O' H. Pratt, com. gun boat Essex, U. S. navy. Died
     Dec. 1863.
Cyrus Fields, Co. C, 53rd Ill. Inf. Died June 9, '85.
John Harvey, Co. A, 53rd Ill. Inf. Died in 1864.
Edward Henning, Co. I, 53rd Ill. Inf. Died July 27, '64.
Chester Martin, Co. — 104th Ill. Inf. Died in 1863.
E. Phelps, Lt. 60th U. S. C. T.
Martin Phelps, Co. E, 53d Ill. Inf. Died in 1881.

Thomas Hickling, Henshaw's Battery.
Clement Luellen, Co. C, 104th Ill. Inf.
H. A. McCobb, Col. 6th U. S. C. T.
Jobey Curtis, Co. A, 64th Ill. Inf. Died Mar. 6th, '64.
C. J. Canders, Co. L. 15th Ill. Inf. Died Jan. 1868,
James C. Cameron, Col. 1st Ala. Cav. Died Apr. 17, '63.
Philip Lundley, capt. and Q. M. 53rd Ill. Inf. Died
    June 25, 1864.
John Flick, sergt. Co, I, 24th Ill. Inf.
Alfred Roberts, Co. E, 104th Ill. Inf. Died Feb. 16, '85.
Thomas Clark, Capt. Co. C, 104th Ill. Inf. Died Jan.
    24, 1883.
William Duckworth, sergt. Cogswell's Battery, Died
    Dec. 22, 1882.
Peter P, Singer, Co. I, 24th Ill. Inf. Died Aug. 10, '80.
Chas. C. Campbell, Lt. Col. 1st Ill. Art. Died July 28, '85.
Chas. Frankenhuser, Co. I, 53rd Ill. Inf. Died Oct.
    10, 1885.
John Reigart, Co. E, 104th Ill. Inf. Died Jan. 23, '68.
Edward Curtis, Co. E, 104th Ill. Died Sept. 11, 1872.
M. D. Lincoln, corp. Co. — 153rd Ill. Inf.
Anton Fink, Co. I, 138th Ill. Inf.
William T. Mancief, sergt. Co. G, 1st Vermont Cav.
P. K. Wilkinson, Co. A, 17th Ill. Inf.
C. P. Clark, chaplain 11th Ill. Inf.
Stephen Nicholson, Cogswell's Battery. Died Jan. 1866.
Miller Barnhardt, corp. Co. B, 53rd Ill. Inf.
John S. Porter, sergt. Co — 138th Ill. Inf.
Albert Schaefer, sergt. Co. I, 24th Ill. Inf. Died in '73.
Louis Matehincky. Corp. H, 4th N. J. Inf. Died Aug.
    23, 1886.
John Schutly, Co. F, 53rd Ill. Inf. Died Nov. 12, '70.
Robt. B. McPherson, Lt. 61st U. S. C. T.
Ira Potter, Cogswell's Battery. Died Nov. 11, '75.
Jacob Weeget, Co. I, 24th Ill. Inf. Died Nov. 25, '83.
B. C. Beebee, capt. Co. — 13th Ind, Inf.
Mark H. Prescott, capt. Co. C, 1st Ill. Art.
Levi R. Black.
Edward Ballman, Co. A, 104th Ill. Inf.
George Hollstern, lieut.
Josiah W. Dean, Co. H, 11th Ill. Inf. Died Apr. 18,
    1884,
Christopher Foster, Co. D, 20th Ill. Inf. Died 1885.
Oliver Cornell, Co. K, 138th Ill. Inf.
John V. Gardner. Died Jan. 7, 1868.
Louis Rendle.
J. W. Bagley, Co. I, 47th Iowa Inf.
Thomas J. Gabler Co. L, 2st N. Y. Art. Died Jan.
    26, 1892.
Geo. A. Balsom, Co. E, 68th Ohio Inf. Died May 25,
    1891.
Chas. McPherson, Co. C, 11th Ill. Cav. Died Oct. 14, '90.
E. B. Beckwith, Co. D, 88th Ill. Inf. Died Jan. 27, '92.
Manley Hill, Cogswell's Battery.
John M. Gill, Lt. Co. — 8th Ill. Inf.

Wesley B. Hall, U. S. navy. Died Dec. 26, 1891.

Wm. H. Lapeer, Co. A, 1st Ill. Art. Died Apr. 3, '92.

Nicholas Tock, Co. E, 12th Ind. Cav. Died Aug. 1892.

Robert Harrington, Cogswell's Battery. Died Feb. 2,
    1893.

Lucien Batchelor, Henshaw's Battery. Died Mar.
    25, 1893.

John Barnhart, Co. E, 64th Ill. Inf.

Iohn B. Merrill, General 64th Ill. Inf. Died July 22,
    1893.

John Burk, Co. C, 76th Ill. Inf. Died July 14, 1893.

Moses Osman, capt. Co. A, 104th Ill. Died Oct. 27, '93.

William Cogswell, Capt. Cogswell's Battery. Died
    Nov. 27, 1893.

William Peckenham. Died in 1893.

Zenas Mann, Co. C, 3rd Wis. Cav. Died Mar. 1, '94.

Joseph E. Skinner, capt. Co. C, 53rd Ill. Inf.

John W. Rhoads, Cos. A and E, 1st Mo. Died June
    18, 1895.

Thos. Barnard, Co. K, 138th Ill. Inf. Died Dec. 31, '83.

Henry J. Read, capt. Co I, 24th Ill. Inf. Died May
    26, 1894.

Henry Vey, Co. A, 77th Pa. Inf. Died Aug. 5, 1894.

David R. Gregg, Co. I, 53rd Ill. Inf. Died Mar. 15, '95.

Thomas Hickling, Co. I, 138th Ill. Inf. Died Dec. 10,
    1893.

Alonson Pope, Co. --- 85th Ill. Inf.

Henry J. Rigdon, Co. K, 12th Ill. Inf. Died Oct. 3, '95.

Reuben F. Dyer, surgeon 104th Ill. Inf. Died Jan. 11,
    1896.

William Gibson, Lt. Col. 4th Ill. Cav. Died Apr. 11, '96.

David Batchelor, Henshaw's Battery. Died Dec. '96.

Fred Stein, Co. C, 1st Ill. Art. Died in 1897.

John Dick, Co. K, 11th and Co. H, 90th Ill. Died June
    20, 1897.

Joseph R. Vance, Co. C, 64th Ill. Inf. Died Nov. 4, '97.

George H. West, Co. L, 15th Ill. Cav. Died Feb. 9, '98.

Hart Norris. Died June, 1897.

Robt. Meheland, Co. C, 3rd Ill. Died May 16, 1898.

Edward Shuler, Co. C, 3rd Ill. Died June 25, 1898.

Silas Alexander, Co. I, 138th Ill Inf.

Joseph Levanery, Co. K, 90th Ill. Inf.

Z. S. Harrison, Co. E, 30th Ill. Inf. Died June 7, '94.

Thomas C. Fullerton, Capt. Co. C, 64th Ill. Inf. Died
    Aug. 2, 1894.

Henry Hodkason, Cogswell's Battery. Died Oct. 9, '98

George Lehr, Co. B, 12th U S. Inf. Died July 1, '98.

Winfield Scott Warren, Co. G, 61st Ill. Died Dec. 24,
    1898.

John F. Read, Co. --- 12th Ill Inf. Died May 6, '99.

Daniel F. Hitt, Col. 53rd Ill. Inf. Died May 6, 1899,

Soldiers of the War of 1812,

Allen Fisher.
Colonel Isaac Dimmick.
John Loyd.
A. W. Caverly. Died Oct. 25, 1876.
Jacob Stroop, Penna. Regt,
Zimri Lewis.
Russel Rathbun.

Soldiers of the Mexican War

Oliver C. Gray, Capt.
Bradford C. Mitchell, 6th U. S. Inf.
Isiah Ackerman, 3rd and 10th U. S. Inf.
Peter Meyer, Co. B, 1st Mo. Art. Died Apr. 22, 1892.
Donat Hallecker.

UNION SOLDIERS BURIED IN THE COLUMBUS CATH-
OLIC CEMETERY; NORTH OTTAWA.

Samuel Ankony, Co. C, 3rd Ohio Cav. Died Nov. 20, 1870.
Thomas Moloney, Co. A, 104th Ill. Inf., died in 1865.
Martin Deveraux, Co. H, 23rd Ill. Inf., died Dec. 17, '70
Patrick Ryder, Henshaw's Battery, died Mar. 18, '82.
John Hanifen, 11th Tennessee Inf., died Feb. 1864.
George Ritter, Co. H, 23d Ill. Inf., died Nov. 1865.
Thomas Ryan, Co. A, 104th Ill., died in 1864.
John Kennedy, Co. K, 53rd Ill. Inf., died Jan. 10, 1881.
Patrick Burkly, capt. Co. K, 53rd Ill. Inf., died June 10, 1881.
Peter Kavanaugh, Orderly to Gen. Grant; died July 13, 1872.
Patrick Ryan, capt. Co. K, 53rd Ill. Inf., died June 14, 1881.
James Graham, Cogswell's Battery, died Sept. 26, '65.
John Cummins. Co. K, 53rd Ill. Inf,, died in 1864.
Michael Leahy, capt. Co. K, 53rd Ill. Inf., died July 12, 1863.
Morris Flynn, Co. H, 23rd Ill. Inf., died in 1880.
James McGowen, 42nd Wis. Inf.
William Coleman, Cogswell's Battery, died Oct. 15, '64.
John White, engineer U. S. navy, died May 5, 1869.
Thomas Brennan, Co. A, 4th Ill. Cav.
Owen Clark, Henshaw's Battery.
Patrick O'Donnell, Co. A, 104th Ill.
Thomas Kennedy, 64th Ill. Inf.
James Harrigan, Co. A, 53rd Ill. Inf., died Mar, 24, '62
Peter Johnson, Co. I, 53rd Ill. Inf., died Oct. 10, '78.
Patrick Stack, Co. K, 90th Ill. Inf., died Dec. 15, '75.
James Busby, Co. H, 23rd Ill. Inf., died Sept. 18, '64.
Patrick Sheridan, Co. K, 90th Ill. Inf., died in 1884.
James Kelly, Co. F, 57th Ill. Inf, died Sept, 15, 1884.
Patrick Dooling, U. S, Navy, died in 1887.

George Hubbard, Cogswell's Battery, died July 21, '68
William McAleer, Co. K, 53rd Ill. Inf.,died Nov. 27, '64.
Jas. McInhill, sergt. Co. H, 23rd Ill. Inf. died May 28, 89
Timothy Donahue, Co. F, 53rd Ill. Inf,, died Apr. 2, '91
James Ferguson, Co. I, 4th and 12th Ill. Cav., died
    Mar. 4, 1891.
William H. Cavin, Cogswell's Battery, died Oct. 10, '91.
John Hammond, Co. H, 11th Ill. Inf., died Nov. '91.
Morris Kerins, Co, K, 53rd Ill. Inf., died July 24, 1891.
Wm. Foley, Co. I, 90th Ill. Inf., died May 1, 1893.
Patrick Kerns, Co. H, 16th U. S. H. A., died Mar. '66.
Thos. Noland, Cogswell's Battery, died Mar. 9, '92.
Timothy O'Connor, Co. A, 104th Ill. Inf,
John Shaunnessy, Co. K, 90th Ill. Inf.
Patrick Holloran, died Nov. 20, 1864.
James Cain, corp. 104th N. Y. Inf., died April 1, '97.
Patrick Shaunnessy, Co. G, 28th Wis. Inf., died Dec.
    18, 1897.
William Mellon, Co. D, 9th Mass. Inf. died Oct. 6, '98.

SOLDIERS BURIED IN SOUTH OTTAWA CEMETERY.

William Meador, died May 15, 1872—war of 1812.
Levi Cummings, war of 1812.
Wm. Teezel, died Sept. 10, 1891—Mexican War.
John Shaw, died Sept. 24, 1874—Florida War.

SOLDIERS BURIED IN BRUMBACK CEMETERY—RUT-
LAND TOWNSHIP.

Edwin A. Boyce, Co. E, 104th Ill., died Mar. 17, '63.
Allen M. Seeman, Co. K, 39th Ill.
A. R. Seeman, Henshaw's Battery.
Sanders Brumback, war of 1812.

SOLDIERS BURIED IN TRUMBO CEMETERY—RUTLAND
TOWNSHIP.

Martin Loy,——Ill. Regt., died in 1892.
Mathias Trumbo,——Va. Inf., war of 1812.

www.ingramcontent.com/pod-product-compliance
Lightning Source LLC
Chambersburg PA
CBHW020241290326
41929CB00045B/1177